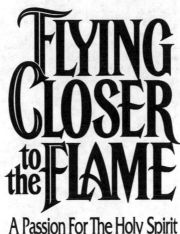

FLYING CLOSER to the FLAME

A Passion For The Holy Spirit

BIBLE STUDY GUIDE

From the Bible-teaching ministry of

Charles R. Swindoll

INSIGHT FOR LIVING

Charles R. Swindoll is a graduate of Dallas Theological Seminary and has served as senior pastor of the First Evangelical Free Church of Fullerton, California, since 1971. Chuck's radio program, "Insight for Living," began in 1979. In addition to his church and radio ministries, Chuck enjoys writing. He has authored numerous books and booklets on a variety of subjects.

Based on the outlines and transcripts of Chuck's sermons, the study guide text is co-authored by Lee Hough, a graduate of the University of Texas at Arlington and Dallas Theological Seminary. He also wrote the Living Insights sections.

Editor in Chief:
Cynthia Swindoll

Coauthor of Text:
Lee Hough

Assistant Editor:
Wendy Peterson

Copy Editors:
Deborah Gibbs
Cheryl Gilmore
Glenda Schlahta

Designer:
Gary Lett

Publishing System Specialist:
Bob Haskins

Director, Communications Division:
Deedee Snyder

Manager, Creative Services:
Alene Cooper

Project Supervisor:
Susan Nelson

Print Production Manager:
John Norton

Printer:
Sinclair Printing Company

Unless otherwise identified, all Scripture references are from the New American Standard Bible, © The Lockman Foundation 1960, 1962, 1963, 1968, 1971, 1972, 1973, 1975, 1977. Used by permission.

Scripture taken from the Holy Bible, New International Version, Copyright © 1973, 1978, 1984 International Bible Society, used by permission of Zondervan Bible Publishers. The other translations cited are the Amplified Bible [AMPLIFIED], the King James Version [KJV], The Living Bible [LB], and the New English Bible [NEB].

An effort has been made to locate sources and obtain permission where necessary for the quotations used in this book. In the event of any unintentional omission, a modification will gladly be incorporated in future printings.

ISBN 0-8499-8476-9
Printed in the United States of America.

CONTENTS

1. This message was not a part of the original series but is compatible with it.

Note

"When the Spirit Brings a Slow Recovery" was not a part of Chuck's original series preached at the church, but was added as a chapter when he wrote the book in May 1993.

INTRODUCTION

The Holy Spirit.

Is there any theological subject more intriguing, more significant . . . or more controversial? Unfortunately, the issues that ought to matter have become little more than fodder for arguments among fellow Christians.

And so . . . I decided to wade right into the middle of it all and take another look—a deeper look—at the One whom Jesus sent to be our Helper. My passion in this study is that we get beyond the theoretical and the "safe" realm and address some of the subjects that truly matter.

The title says it all: flying closer to the flame is not only my subject, it is our great need. Long enough have we evangelicals kept our distance from the blessed Spirit of God! Long enough have we allowed our fears to restrain us! I am firmly convinced that one need not be a "charismatic Christian" in order to tap into God's power.

Without losing our strong theological moorings, we shall move nearer than ever to the things of the Spirit. Hopefully, the unusually intimate pursuit of the truth will open new eyes and warm cold hearts. By God's grace, we shall discover fresh dimensions of the One who was sent to transform our lives.

Chuck Swindoll

Chuck Swindoll

PUTTING TRUTH
INTO ACTION

Knowledge apart from application falls short of God's desire for His children. He wants us to apply what we learn so that we will change and grow. This study guide was prepared with these goals in mind. As you go through the following pages, we hope your desire to discover biblical truth will grow as your understanding of God's Word increases, and that you will be encouraged to apply what you've learned.

To assist you in your study, we've included a section called ♦ **Living Insights** at the end of each lesson. These exercises will challenge you to study further and to think of specific ways to put your discoveries into action.

There are many ways to use this guide—in personal devotions, group studies, discussions with friends and family, and Sunday school classes. And, of course, it's an ideal study aid when you're listening to its corresponding "Insight for Living" radio series.

To benefit most from this study guide, we would encourage you to consider it a spiritual journal. That's why we've included space in the **Living Insights** for recording your thoughts and discoveries. We hope you'll return to those sections often for review and encouragement as you continue to grow in your walk with Christ.

Lee Hough
Coauthor of Text
Author of Living Insights

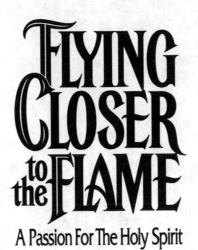

A Passion For The Holy Spirit

Chapter 1

LET'S GET REACQUAINTED WITH THE SPIRIT

Selected Scriptures

Winston Churchill once described Russia as "a riddle wrapped in a mystery inside an enigma."[1] How many of us, I wonder, would say the same thing about the Holy Spirit? Be truthful now. Put away all the textbook definitions, and think about what you really know about Him.

The fact is, many Christians have never really understood Him well at all, and that lack of understanding is reflected in our awkward attempts to relate to Him. At best, we might say that our relationship is an uncomfortable one. We're not sure what to say or feel or how to act around Him, so we often ignore Him as if He were an uninvited member of the Trinity. Then, too, He often gets credited for people's bizarre behavior, which only increases our fears. The end result is that, instead of drawing closer to God's Spirit, many believers back away with a wary attitude.

Could it be that insecurity and guardedness are keeping you from getting acquainted with God's intimate Spirit? He is that, you know . . . intimate, personal, and penetratingly practical. So c'mon, don't be shy. Come up close and get to know this companion of our souls who strengthens and guides us on our spiritual journey. Let your heart be warmed by the flame of His empowering presence.

Ready?

Then let's begin by calling on Him with this simple yet eloquent prayer.

---

1. Winston Churchill, as quoted in *Bartlett's Familiar Quotations*, 15th ed., rev. and enl., ed. Emily Morison Beck (Boston, Mass.: Little, Brown and Co., 1980), p. 743.

> Come, Holy Ghost, our souls inspire,
> And lighten us with celestial fire.[2]

Blowing the Dust off "The Ghost"

With so many of us feeling confused about who the Spirit is and what He does, perhaps it would be helpful if we identified some of the key reasons for our bewilderment.

Removing the Mysterious-Secret Mentality

Since we're all familiar with earthly fathers, it's relatively easy to grasp the concept of God as our heavenly Father. Then, too, we can readily identify with Jesus, God's Son, because He took on human flesh and lived as one of us for thirty-three years. But the Spirit—the "Holy Ghost," as He is sometimes called—how are we supposed to understand what that means?

Another source of confusion has to do with our understanding of the roles assigned to each member of the Trinity. The Father is clearly portrayed in the Scriptures as sovereignly in control, the planner of all things. He planned our salvation, for example, and His Son implemented that plan with His life, death, and resurrection. So with salvation already planned and performed, what need or function is left for the Holy Spirit to fill?

Last, sound biblical teaching on the Father and the Son abounds. By comparison, however, the Holy Spirit seems virtually neglected. And even when He is taught, the approach is usually a dry theological exercise rather than a vibrant personal discovery. Is it any wonder, then, why we tend to treat the Spirit more like a stranger and an outsider than a friend?

Where Are We Going in This Study?

Our goal in this series is not to simply study God's Spirit, but to embrace Him. And to do that, we'll be focusing on the more intimate and personal dimensions of His work in us. For example:

In Ephesians 5:18, we'll examine what it means to be "filled with the Spirit."

In Acts 1:8, we'll explore the empowering of the Spirit.

In 1 Corinthians 2:9–13, we'll consider how He "searches . . . the depths of God" and how He reveals these things to us.

---

2. Rabanus Maurus, as quoted in *12,000 Religious Quotations*, comp. Frank S. Mead (1965; reprint, Grand Rapids, Mich.: Baker Book House, 1989), p. 228.

In 1 John 2:18–20, we'll ask what the Spirit's "anointing" means.

Granted, our attempts to draw out the meaning of these things won't be easy. The terms describing His work are often vague and marginally explained. But rather than run in fright from the unknown as so many do, our goal will be to tenaciously grapple with each facet of His ministry, (like Jacob with the angel), refusing to let go until the Spirit blesses us with a deeper, clearer understanding of Himself.

Discovering the Spirit's Significance

Attempting to know the Spirit on a more personal level instead of just a cognitive one will undoubtedly make some of you nervous. You may be frightened that this path will lead to some sort of experiential mysticism. If this is your concern, relax—we're not suggesting we leave the sure footing of the Scriptures in our attempt to become more closely acquainted with the Holy Spirit. It's what God's Word reveals about the Spirit that we seek, and we needn't be afraid of allowing that truth to deepen our awareness and intimacy with Him.

Having said that, let's begin our journey of discovery now by examining three essential truths concerning the Spirit's significance.

His Permanent Presence within Us

Our first passage, John 14, takes us to the upper room of a first-century home in Jerusalem where Jesus and His disciples are celebrating Passover. Christ knows that the hour has come for His arrest and crucifixion, so He tells Peter, John, and the rest that He will be leaving them soon. The disciples immediately pale at the frightening thought of losing Jesus. What will they do? Where will they go? So the Master offers them these words of comfort and counsel.

> "Let not your heart be troubled; believe in God, believe also in Me. In My Father's house are many dwelling places; if it were not so, I would have told you; for I go to prepare a place for you. And if I go and prepare a place for you, I will come again, and receive you to Myself; that where I am, there you may be also. And you know the way where I am going." Thomas said to Him, "Lord, we do not know where You are going, how do we know the way?"

3

Jesus said to him, "I am the way, and the truth, and the life; no one comes to the Father, but through Me." (vv. 1–6)

These familiar words may have little emotional impact on us today, but imagine the great turmoil they caused the disciples. For the past three years—and for all eternity, the disciples thought—Jesus had been their constant companion. Now He's abandoning them? Suddenly this small group of grown men feels like lost and helpless children.

Sensing their confusion and need for still more encouragement, Jesus tells them,

"Truly, truly, I say to you, he who believes in Me, the works that I do shall he do also; and greater works than these shall he do; because I go to the Father." (v. 12)

"We're going to do greater works than You, Lord? Impossible!" the disciples must have thought. "We could never accomplish such great things on our own." And they're right; by themselves they can't, which is why Jesus goes on to introduce them to the One who will make these things possible.

"And I will ask the Father, and He will give you another Helper, that He may be with you forever; that is the Spirit of truth, whom the world cannot receive, because it does not behold Him or know Him, but you know Him because He abides with you, and will be in you." (vv. 16–17)

Up until now, the Spirit had been with them, abiding *alongside* them. Very soon, however, He would be *in* them! A whole new relationship was about to begin that would transform these frightened fishermen into bold fishers of men. And notice the last word in verse 16—"forever." The Holy Spirit was coming to stay. His presence would be permanently fixed in their innermost being. No more would He come just to accomplish special tasks and then be withdrawn, as in the Old Testament days.[3] He was coming to stay. Incredible!

3. For further study, see Numbers 11:16–17, 25; Judges 14:5–6, 19; 15:14; 1 Samuel 10:9–11; 16:14; Psalm 51:11.

But when, exactly, would all this take place? A little later in that same conversation, Jesus tells the disciples,

> "I tell you the truth, it is to your advantage that I go away; for if I do not go away, the Helper shall not come to you; but if I go, I will send Him to you." (16:7)

The Spirit's arrival required Jesus' departure. So let's move ahead to that moment in Acts 1 when, after His death and resurrection, Jesus gathered the disciples to say good-bye and give them some final instructions regarding the Spirit.

His Unparalleled Dynamic among Us

> And gathering them together, He commanded them not to leave Jerusalem, but to wait for what the Father had promised, "Which," He said, "you heard of from Me; for John baptized with water, but you shall be baptized with the Holy Spirit not many days from now."
>
> And so when they had come together, they were asking Him, saying, "Lord, is it at this time You are restoring the kingdom to Israel?" He said to them, "It is not for you to know times or epochs which the Father has fixed by His own authority; but you shall receive power when the Holy Spirit has come upon you; and you shall be My witnesses both in Jerusalem, and in all Judea and Samaria, and even to the remotest part of the earth." (Acts 1:4–8)

"Wait for the Holy Spirit," Jesus told them, "wait for the power. He's coming and He brings with Him a *dunamis*," translated *dynamic*, "that will enable you to come out from hiding behind closed doors and be powerful witnesses throughout the world" (see John 20:19). Commentator F. F. Bruce writes,

> Instead of the political power which had formerly been the object of their ambitions, a power far greater and nobler would be theirs. When the Holy Spirit came upon them, Jesus assured them, they would be clothed with heavenly power—that power by which . . . their mighty works were accomplished and their preaching made effective. As Jesus Himself had been anointed at His baptism with

5

the Holy Spirit and power, so His followers were now to be similarly anointed and enabled to carry on His work.[4]

Think of it. All of us who know Christ are indwelt by this same incredible Person and power. We, too, have His unparalleled dynamism available to help us carry on as Christ's witnesses. And to confirm that truth, let's move ahead in the Scriptures once again to those days after the Spirit's arrival and briefly highlight a few examples of His power at work in the disciples.

His Affirming Will for Us

Jesus promised the disciples that the Holy Spirit would empower them to be His witnesses to the world, and that's exactly what we see happening upon the Spirit's arrival in Acts 2. He filled the Twelve, and they immediately began proclaiming the gospel in the different dialects of the people gathered in Jerusalem. By the end of that first day, about three thousand people had been saved (vv. 1–41).

Opposition steadily grew from the religious rulers of their day, but the Holy Spirit strengthened the disciples to persevere in their witnessing. Eventually, Peter and John were arrested and arraigned before Israel's supreme court, with the high priest presiding. Rather than feeling intimidated and afraid, however, Peter and John demonstrated a boldness that amazed even their accusers.[5]

> Now as they observed the confidence of Peter and
> John, and understood that they were uneducated
> and untrained men, they were marveling, and began
> to recognize them as having been with Jesus. (4:13)

Another follower of Christ whom the Spirit empowered to witness, to persevere under persecution, and to face his accusers with confidence was Stephen. In the final moments before his martyrdom, he also exhibited the Spirit's grace and power to endure unjust suffering with a forgiving attitude (7:51–60).

These are but a few examples of the Holy Spirit's transforming presence that is still available, still active in believers today. So why

---

4. F. F. Bruce, *Commentary on the Book of the Acts*, 3d ed. (London, England: Marshall, Morgan and Scott, 1962), pp. 38–39.

5. See also Acts 5:28–29, 41–42.

do some of us see so little of His presence in our lives? Perhaps because of a few old habits that put barriers between us and Him.

Removing the Resistance between Us and Him

Three habits in particular that block many Christians from knowing the Spirit more intimately are, first, *the barrier of the fearful unknown*. Granted, the Holy Spirit is not Someone we can dissect with our doctrines until we discover all there is to know about Him. But that shouldn't make us afraid of Him. Don't fear the unknown, a deeper understanding of who He is and what He does. Fear only that which is not true.

Second, *the wall of traditional limitations*. Jaroslav Pelikan once wrote, "Tradition is the living faith of those now dead; traditionalism is the dead faith of those now living."[6] Those of us caught up in traditionalism naturally resist the Holy Spirit because He is the author of change, and that frightens lovers of conformity and sameness.

And third, *the obstacle course of personal excuses*. The truth is, we're all as close to the Holy Spirit as we choose to be. Unfortunately, what some of us choose are excuses instead of intimacy. We would rather hide behind theological quibblings where we feel safe than risk reaching out to know Him in a more personal way.

Is it possible that you're blocking yourself from knowing the Spirit more closely because of one of these barriers? Let's explore that question a little more deeply in the first Living Insight.

 Living Insights   STUDY ONE

The fact that you're even reading this study guide is an indication that you desire to know the Spirit better. And that's good! But perhaps one or more of the barriers described in this chapter are holding you back. Can you identify them? Better still, can you put your finger on the specific thoughts and feelings that make up the bricks of that barrier? Use the space provided to describe them as accurately as you can. And don't shy away from putting down everything that comes to your mind—no matter how farfetched or ridiculous it may seem.

---

6. As quoted by Charles R. Swindoll in *Living Above the Level of Mediocrity* (Waco, Tex.: Word Books, Publisher, 1987), p. 163.

The Barrier of the Fearful Unknown

_____

_____

_____

The Wall of Traditional Resistance

_____

_____

_____

The Hurdle of Personal Excuses

_____

_____

_____

Other

_____

_____

_____

As you've probably already realized, putting your thoughts and feelings down on paper makes it easier to discern the real barriers from the ridiculous. Are there some you can easily remove? As for the others, they will obviously take more time. But it's our hope that as you continue your journey in the following chapters, you'll learn along the way how to dismantle these barriers and draw close to the Holy Spirit.

Living Insights

The goal of this study guide is not just to gain more head knowledge but to develop a deeper understanding of and intimacy with the Spirit. So let's start by sketching a verbal picture of what we honestly think and feel about who He is and how we relate to Him. Then, at the conclusion of this guide, we'll compose another verbal sketch and compare the two to see how you've been able to see and know Him better.

Sketch

_____

_____

_____

_____

_____

_____

_____

_____

_____

_____

_____

_____

_____

_____

_____

_____

Chapter 2

THE MAIN AGENDA OF GOD'S SPIRIT: TRANSFORMATION

Selected Scriptures

Were you there? Did you see it? Oh . . . of course not, you couldn't have. It all happened so long ago. But I tell you something did happen on that day, something incredible! A power was loosed that suddenly shook the world, split hardened hearts, and tore the veil of spiritual darkness in people's souls from top to bottom.

Oh, if only you could have been there. You would have heard the thundering voices of twelve transformed men take a throng of thousands by storm. With unexpected fluency, they proclaimed in the diverse languages of the people a single, powerful message:

> "Let all the house of Israel know for certain that God has made Him both Lord and Christ—this Jesus whom you crucified." (Acts 2:36)

Those words struck a spark of repentance that caught the tinder of the Spirit's presence and quickly spread through the multitude like a flame. And the disciples fanned that flame with their impassioned witnessing.

Amazed, bewildered, marveled—these words describe the people's reaction to the dynamic displayed in those twelve men on the day of Pentecost. If only we could have been there to see it for ourselves.

But wait, perhaps we still can! Let's go back with the Scripture's help and compare what the disciples were like before and after the Spirit's arrival. Then we'll see, almost as clearly as if we had been in that crowd ourselves, the transformation that took place in the lives of the Twelve.

A Brief Glance at the "Orphaned" Disciples

Our first task is to get a clear picture of what the disciples were like before Pentecost—and that may not be too easy. For the perception firmly fixed in many of our minds is shaped more by the stained-glass images in our churches than by reality. So let's see if we can adjust our picture until the real flesh-and-blood followers of Jesus come into focus.

Who They Were

In his book *The Master Plan of Evangelism*, Robert Coleman shatters any haloed misconceptions we may have about who the disciples were with this more accurate description:

> What is more revealing about these men is that at first they do not impress us as being key men. None of them occupied prominent places in the Synagogue, nor did any of them belong to the Levitical priesthood. For the most part they were common laboring men, probably having no professional training beyond the rudiments of knowledge necessary for their vocation. Perhaps a few of them came from families of some considerable means, such as the sons of Zebedee, but none of them could have been considered wealthy. They had no academic degrees in the arts and philosophies of their day. Like their Master, their formal education likely consisted only of the Synagogue schools. Most of them were raised in the poor section of the country around Galilee. Apparently the only one of the twelve who came from the more refined region of Judea was Judas Iscariot. By any standard of sophisticated culture then and now they would surely be considered as a rather ragged aggregation of souls. One might wonder how Jesus could ever use them. They were impulsive, temperamental, easily offended, and had all the prejudices of their environment. In short, these men selected by the Lord to be His assistants represented an average cross section of the lot of society in their day. Not the kind of group one would expect to win the world for Christ.[1]

Can you see the disciples a little more clearly now? Is your focus better? That's good. But let's fine-tune it even further by examining

---

1. Robert E. Coleman, *The Master Plan of Evangelism*, 2d ed. (Old Tappan, N.J.: Fleming H. Revell Co., 1964), pp. 22–23.

how they felt just before Christ's death and on the day of His ascension.

How They Felt

> "Little children, I am with you a little while longer. You shall seek Me; and as I said to the Jews, I now say to you also, 'Where I am going, you cannot come.'" (John 13:33)

Jesus spoke these disturbing words when He was with the disciples in the Upper Room on the night of His betrayal. He had tried before to prepare them for His arrest and crucifixion, but until now they had refused to let it sink in. Finally, Peter senses the seriousness of what He's saying and responds with, "Lord, why can I not follow You right now? I will lay down my life for You" (v. 37). But Jesus replies,

> "Will you lay down your life for Me? Truly, truly, I say to you, a cock shall not crow, until you deny Me three times." (v. 38)

Undoubtedly, that statement shocked the rest of the disciples and devastated Peter. They were already feeling unsettled by Jesus' accusation that one of them would betray Him. And now this? He's leaving and Peter will deny Him? Everything dear that defined their world, gave them hope and security, was suddenly falling apart.

It's in the midst of this distressing meal that we can begin to see with intimate clarity the contours of the disciples' frail humanity. First, we see from Jesus' next words that they were deeply *troubled*.

> "Let not your heart be troubled; believe in God, believe also in Me." (14:1)

Second, they were *confused*. When Jesus said they knew the way to the place He was preparing for them, Thomas replied, "Lord, we do not know where You are going, how do we know the way?" (v. 5). And then a little later in this same conversation, some of the disciples looked at each other in bewilderment and said,

> "What is this thing He is telling us, 'A little while, and you will not behold Me; and again a little while, and you will see Me'; and, 'because I go to the Father'?" And so they were saying, "What is this that He says, 'A little while'? We do not know what

He is talking about." (16:17–18)

Third, they felt *abandoned*. Jesus' talk of leaving absolutely frightened them, and He knew that. So He reached out to calm their fears with the reassurance, "I will not leave you as orphans; I will come to you" (14:18).

Fourth, as we've already noted, they felt *afraid*. Again Christ's words amplify the pounding hearts of the disciples.

"Peace I leave with you; My peace I give to you; not as the world gives, do I give to you. Let not your heart be troubled, nor let it be fearful." (14:27)

Fifth, they felt *intimidated*. Matthew tells us that later that same night, as the Roman cohort and the officers of the chief priests and the Pharisees came to arrest Christ, "all the disciples left Him and fled" (Matthew 26:56; see also John 20:19).

And sixth, they felt *unsure, lacking in understanding*. Even after His death and resurrection, up to the last moment before Jesus ascended into heaven, the disciples still couldn't grasp the big picture concerning the future.

And gathering them together, He commanded them not to leave Jerusalem, but to wait for what the Father had promised, "Which," He said, "you heard of from Me; for John baptized with water, but you shall be baptized with the Holy Spirit not many days from now."

And so when they had come together, they were asking Him, saying, "Lord, is it at this time You are restoring the kingdom to Israel?" (Acts 1:4–6)

Weak, intimidated, vacillating, confused—combined, these give us a true portrait of what the disciples were like in those final days prior to the coming of the Holy Spirit. Now let's compare this to the picture we see of them on the day of Pentecost and immediately thereafter.

An Enlightening Discovery of Personal Transformation

And when the day of Pentecost had come, they were all together in one place. And suddenly there came from heaven a noise like a violent, rushing wind, and it filled the whole house where they were sitting. And there appeared to them tongues as of fire distributing themselves, and they rested on each one of them. And they were all filled with the Holy Spirit. (2:1–4a)

It was an unforgettable moment, a dividing line in the disciples' lives. In that juncture of furious sound and fire, a transformation took place that brought about no less than four undeniable changes.

First, *the disciples' human frailties were transformed into supernatural gifts and abilities*. We see this happening immediately upon the Spirit's arrival, as they "began to speak with other tongues, as the Spirit was giving them utterance" (v. 4b).

Now there were Jews living in Jerusalem, devout men, from every nation under heaven. And when this sound occurred, the multitude came together, and were bewildered, because they were each one hearing them speak in his own language. And they were amazed and marveled, saying, "Why, are not all these who are speaking Galileans? And how is it that we each hear them in our own language to which we were born? Parthians and Medes and Elamites, and residents of Mesopotamia, Judea and Cappadocia, Pontus and Asia, Phrygia and Pamphylia, Egypt and the districts of Libya around Cyrene, and visitors from Rome, both Jews and proselytes, Cretans and Arabs—we hear them in our own tongues speaking of the mighty deeds of God." (vv. 5–11)

Another demonstration of supernatural gifting by the Spirit occurs in Acts 3, where Peter and John heal a man lame from birth. The people were amazed by this miraculous display of power. But rather than pretend the power came from themselves, Peter turned the people to its true source.

"Men of Israel, why do you marvel at this, or why do you gaze at us, as if by our own power or piety we had made him walk? The God of Abraham, Isaac, and Jacob, the God of our fathers, has glorified His servant Jesus. . . . And on the basis of faith in His name, it is the name of Jesus which has strengthened this man whom you see and know; and the faith which comes through Him has given him this perfect health in the presence of you all." (vv. 12–13a, 16)

Second, *the disciples' fearful reluctance was transformed into bold confidence*. Not only did they unabashedly take to the streets to proclaim the gospel, but when people began mocking them, Peter boldly stood up and preached a defense that pierced his hecklers to the heart (see 2:13–36). And when they begged him, "What shall we do?" he answered,

> "Repent, and let each of you be baptized in the name of Jesus Christ for the forgiveness of your sins; and you shall receive the gift of the Holy Spirit. For the promise is for you and your children, and for all who are far off, as many as the Lord our God shall call to Himself." And with many other words he solemnly testified and kept on exhorting them, saying, "Be saved from this perverse generation!" So then, those who had received his word were baptized; and there were added that day about three thousand souls. (2:38–41)

Can there be any doubt about the transforming power of the Holy Spirit when you compare this Peter to the one who abandoned Jesus at His arrest, denied Him three times, and hid behind locked doors for fear of persecution from the very people he was now leading to Christ?

Recall, too, from our last chapter, how even the religious leaders who opposed Peter were amazed by the confidence they saw in him (4:1–13).

Third, *the disciples' fears and intimidation were transformed into a sense of invincibility*. Peter and John were arrested for preaching Christ and arraigned before the Sanhedrin, who then tried to threaten and intimidate them so they would stop witnessing.

> And when they had summoned them, they commanded them not to speak or teach at all in the name of Jesus. (4:18)

This was Israel's supreme ruling authority, made up of its highest religious leaders, ordering Peter and John to cease and desist all preaching. But even after spending a night in jail, these two Spirit-filled disciples weren't the least bit intimidated.

But Peter and John answered and said to them,

"Whether it is right in the sight of God to give heed to you rather than to God, you be the judge; for we cannot stop speaking what we have seen and heard." (vv. 19–20)

As you read of this whole incident in Acts 4, from beginning to end you'll find that it was the religious leaders who were "disturbed" and intimidated, not Peter and John.

Fourth, *the disciples' lonely, grim feelings of abandonment were transformed into joyful perseverance.* Peter and John, as well as the rest of the disciples, were arrested on another occasion and taken before the Sanhedrin. This time, instead of just ordering them to stop witnessing, the religious court fined them with a flogging (v. 40). But did this stop them? Did it cause them to feel resentful and abandoned by Jesus? See for yourself.

They went on their way from the presence of the Council, rejoicing that they had been considered worthy to suffer shame for His name. And every day, in the temple and from house to house, they kept right on teaching and preaching Jesus as the Christ. (5:41–42)

Incredible, isn't it? These men who once scurried from house to house like frightened mice had suddenly become roaring lions, tenacious and unafraid even in the midst of persecution.

A Straightforward Analysis of How It Happened

That something happened to the disciples which brought about an amazing transformation is clear. We would attribute it to the Holy Spirit, based on the authority of the Scriptures. But others might put the credit somewhere else. Let's briefly consider some other explanations, gaining a better understanding of why they won't hold up and why only the Holy Spirit's transforming power will.

Possible Options

Perhaps it was positive thinking that changed the disciples. After Christ ascended, maybe they just decided it was time to grow up and be responsible. Sounds pretty weak, don't you think? Positive thinking can never instantly transform a person who is intimidated, confused, and afraid into someone who is bold and invincible. Besides, it is very doubtful that positive thinking could ever empower someone to rejoice after having his or her back shredded by a whip.

Another possibility is a better environment. It could be that the disciples changed simply because the Jews in Jerusalem became more open and willing to accept the blame for crucifying Christ. Wrong! The fact is, just the opposite was true. Opposition grew more and more intense.

What about mutual encouragement? Well, how would people who were all afraid and intimidated muster up the strength to encourage another? It doesn't seem likely, does it?

Who knows, maybe they all enrolled in a class on how to be more assertive! Now we're slipping into the ridiculous. No, there's only one plausible answer.

Best (and Only) Conclusion

The best answer is found in Acts 1:8.

> "But you shall receive power when the Holy Spirit has come upon you; and you shall be My witnesses both in Jerusalem, and in all Judea and Samaria, and even to the remotest part of the earth."

If it had not been for the Holy Spirit filling the disciples, those twelve men could have easily passed into history without leaving any mark on the first-century world. They were ordinary human beings, just like the rest of us. But they accomplished something extraordinary because of the supernatural transforming Spirit of God that empowered them.

A Probing Question Only You Can Answer

Were you there? Did you see the transformation that took place in the disciples that day? We hope this study has enabled you to glimpse with first-century eyes the powerful changes that occurred. More than that, we hope you'll realize that the same Holy Spirit who empowered the disciples that day filled you as well the moment you believed in Jesus. With each conversion, the drama of the Spirit coming to empower another life reoccurs. How He will transform you is a story that only you and He can write.

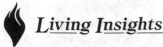

In the preface to his book *The Mystery of the Holy Spirit*, R. C. Sproul writes:

> "The Holy Spirit leaves no footprints in the sand." These words are from Abraham Kuyper's classic work on the Holy Spirit. Jesus did leave footprints in the sand. He was God incarnate, God with a human nature. When His disciples walked with Him, they could hear His voice, touch His hands, and watch the sand spilling over His feet as He trod the shores of the Sea of Galilee.
>
> But the Holy Spirit is like the wind. Jesus said, "The wind blows where it wishes, and you hear the sound of it, but cannot tell where it comes from and where it goes" (John 3:8). We cannot capture the wind in a bottle. It is elusive and mysterious but nonetheless real. We see the effects of the wind— trees bending and swaying in the breeze, flags rustling. We see the devastation of the fierce hurricane. We see the ocean become violent in a gale. We are refreshed by gentle zephyrs on a summer day. We know the wind is there.
>
> So it is with the Holy Spirit. He is intangible and invisible. But His work is more powerful than the most ferocious wind. The Spirit brings order out of chaos and beauty out of ugliness. He can transform a sin-blistered man into a paragon of virtue. The Spirit changes people. The Author of life is also the Transformer of life.[2]

What evidence of the Spirit's transforming presence can people see in your life? What effects have you noticed? Is it possible that you have grown lax in appreciating all that He does? Many of us have. In truth, we take the Holy Spirit for granted. We just expect Him to work without taking the time or effort to see what He's doing or to thank the Father for it.

2. R. C. Sproul, *The Mystery of the Holy Spirit* (Wheaton, Ill.: Tyndale House Publishers, 1990), p. 7.

Let's take this opportunity to deepen our awareness and appreciation of His work in our lives. Think back to what you were like before you were a Christian and compare that to what you have become since. If you need help being specific, examine the fruits of the flesh and the Spirit contrasted in Galatians 5:19–23.

Before

_____

_____

_____

_____

_____

After

_____

_____

_____

_____

_____

 Living Insights _____ STUDY TWO

The disciples had many weaknesses. But, like the apostle Paul, they learned that God's grace is sufficient, that His power is perfected in weakness. "Therefore I am well content with weaknesses," Paul wrote,

> with insults, with distresses, with persecutions, with difficulties, for Christ's sake; for when I am weak, then I am strong. (2 Cor. 12:10)

What particular weaknesses must you trust the Holy Spirit to make strong?

1. _____

2. _____

3._____

Is there a particular one right now that you're not trusting Him for?

_____

_____

_____

Like Paul, admit your weakness to the Lord and pray for His strength to be perfected in this particular area.

Chapter 3

MY SIN . . . AND "THE THINGS OF THE SPIRIT"
Romans 8

This chapter is not for the timid or the weak. If you hate conflict and want to avoid it, perhaps it would be best if you didn't pursue finding out what the "things of the Spirit" are. Because to achieve that objective, you must first pass through a war zone unlike any you've ever heard or read about in the news—one whose co-ordinates you won't find on any map. For the field of battle lies in the uncharted spiritual realm of the soul.

For those of you intrepid enough to seek the answer, read on to one veteran's account of the inner firefight. But don't think it's limited to him; this battle is happening right now inside every believer's heart between the forces of good and evil, the Spirit and the flesh.

An Understanding of the Context of Romans 8

The apostle Paul camps for some time in the beginning of his letter to the Romans on the cause of all our conflict—sin. This enemy of the soul has destroyed our innocence with depravity and desolated our lives with death. For three hopeless chapters, the Apostle reconnoiters the wickedness of our corrupted natures. Then, in chapters 4–5, he introduces Jesus Christ as the One whose death has liberated us from sin's dark domination. But our battle with sin isn't over yet . . .

The good news in Romans 6 is that *sin no longer has the power over us*. From the moment of salvation, we have been emancipated from our slavery to sin to become servants of righteousness.

> Therefore do not let sin reign in your mortal body that you should obey its lusts, and do not go on presenting the members of your body to sin as instruments of unrighteousness; but present your-selves to God as those alive from the dead, and your members as instruments of righteousness to God. For sin shall not be master over you, for you are not under law, but under grace. (vv. 12–14)

According to Romans 7, however, *sin is still present within us*. It constantly fights to wrest control of our hearts and minds from our new Master. And it often succeeds—with our help, as the exasperated author admits.

> For that which I am doing, I do not understand; for
> I am not practicing what I would like to do, but I
> am doing the very thing I hate. . . . Wretched man
> that I am! Who will set me free from the body of
> this death? (vv. 15, 24)

The answer Paul seeks, one we all desperately need, is found in the exciting news of Romans 8: *The Spirit provides a new dimension of living*. By ourselves, we cannot conquer the sin that indwells us. But now, with the Holy Spirit residing in our hearts, we have the necessary reinforcement to overcome sin so that we may live for Christ.

My Flesh . . . His Spirit

With both our sin nature (the "flesh," as it is called in Romans 7) and the Spirit entrenched within us, a furious war is constantly waged within our soul.

The Struggles Every Christian Goes Through

For a closer look at this conflict, let's turn to Galatians 5, where Paul identifies the two battlefronts on which this war is actually fought. First, there is the *external* arena.

> For you were called to freedom, brethren; only
> do not turn your freedom into an opportunity for
> the flesh, but through love serve one another. For
> the whole Law is fulfilled in one word, in the state-
> ment, "You shall love your neighbor as yourself." But
> if you bite and devour one another, take care lest
> you be consumed by one another. (vv. 13–15)

Sarcasm, gossip, selfishness—these are just a few of the visible struggles that take place among Christians. We can hear the bullets of bitter words as they explode from people's lips; we can see the devastation caused by greed, pride, and lust. Marriages are wiped out, children are maimed, unborn babies are slaughtered, people are starved and abused, livelihoods are destroyed, and relationships are left in rubble, just to name a few.

Much more subtle, but just as real, is the second realm of struggle described in Galatians 5—the *internal* arena.

> But I say, walk by the Spirit, and you will not carry out the desire of the flesh. For the flesh sets its desire against the Spirit, and the Spirit against the flesh; for these are in opposition to one another, so that you may not do the things that you please. (vv. 16–17)

The Living Bible gives this helpful rendition of verse 17:

> For we naturally love to do evil things that are just the opposite from the things that the Holy Spirit tells us to do; and the good things we want to do when the Spirit has his way with us are just the opposite of our natural desires. These two forces within us are constantly fighting each other to win control over us, and our wishes are never free from their pressures.

In the Amplified Bible, the center part of this verse says that the Spirit and the flesh "are antagonistic to each other [continually withstanding and in conflict with each other]." Inside every believer is a battle royal between the sinful cravings of the flesh and the righteous desires of the Spirit. But because these two clash in a realm where we cannot see or hear the terrible fighting, we often forget that it is even happening. We take for granted that God's Spirit is locked in a deadly struggle for us, that every moment of every day He grapples with this lethal enemy that seeks to destroy our life.

Now, some of you may be thinking that this sounds a little melodramatic. Surely with the Spirit of God in us, the influence of the flesh can't be that great, can it?

You decide.

When the Flesh Is Dominant

Paul has already told us that Christians constantly face internal and external struggles with the flesh. Now he takes us on an unpleasant tour of the destructive behavior the flesh leaves in its path.

> Now the deeds of the flesh are evident, which are: immorality, impurity, sensuality, idolatry, sorcery, enmities, strife, jealousy, outbursts of anger, disputes,

dissensions, factions, envying, drunkenness, carousing, and things like these, of which I forewarn you just as I have forewarned you that those who practice such things shall not inherit the kingdom of God. (vv. 19–21)

What Paul describes here is the lifestyle of the lost person, not the Christian. To make that clear, he uses the tense for *practice* which means "habitually practices." In other words, he's describing someone whose life isn't just occasionally marked by these sins but is consumed by them their entire lives. But when the flesh dominates the believer's life, these sins can and will reemerge at times. Sometimes so much so, in fact, that you might think an individual is unsaved!

When the Spirit Takes Control

In contrast, when the Spirit is in control, a new nature emerges that is wholesome and healthy.

But the fruit of the Spirit is love, joy, peace, patience, kindness, goodness, faithfulness, gentleness, self-control; against such things there is no law. (vv. 22–23)

The choice is ours. We can, as Paul says in Romans 8:5, set our "minds on the things of the flesh" or we can set them on the magnificent "things of the Spirit." We will become the follower of whichever master we choose to obey, as Paul clearly affirms:

Do you not know that when you present yourselves to someone as slaves for obedience, you are slaves of the one whom you obey, either of sin resulting in death, or of obedience resulting in righteousness? (Rom. 6:16)

In Romans 8, Paul gives us even more specifics regarding the righteous "things of the Spirit" that are reproduced in us when we are under His control. For example,

- Life and peace—"For the mind set on the flesh is death, but the mind set on the Spirit is life and peace" (8:6).

- Absence of fear and closeness to God—"For you have not received a spirit of slavery leading to fear again, but you have received a spirit of adoption as sons by which we cry out, 'Abba! Father!'" (v. 15).

- Inner feelings of assurance . . . doubts gone!—"The Spirit Himself bears witness with our spirit that we are children of God, and if children, heirs also, heirs of God and fellow heirs with Christ, if indeed we suffer with Him in order that we may also be glorified with Him" (vv. 16–17).

- Assistance in prayer—"And in the same way the Spirit also helps our weakness; for we do not know how to pray as we should, but the Spirit Himself intercedes for us with groanings too deep for words; and He who searches the hearts knows what the mind of the Spirit is, because He intercedes for the saints according to the will of God" (vv. 26–27).

- Inner "awareness" that all things are working together for good and God's glory—"And we know that God causes all things to work together for good to those who love God, to those who are called according to His purpose" (v. 28).

Three Absolutely Thrilling Thoughts

As we conclude our time in the trenches with the Spirit, here are three thoughts to encourage you in your pursuit of the "things of the Spirit."

First, *there are realms of earthly experience we have never traveled,* which the Spirit can open up to us.

Second, *there are depths of God's will we have never tapped,* which the Spirit wants to show us.

Third, *there are dimensions of supernatural power we have never touched,* which the Spirit will allow within us.

Doesn't it excite you to know that you have such an incredible ally in your fight against the flesh? Someone who will never desert you, never abandon His post on the front line of your heart, where you're the most vulnerable?

How about letting Him know that right now. Give Him the praise and thanks He deserves. He'll be excited too—about you.

 Living Insights STUDY ONE

To gain a deeper appreciation of and perspective on the "things of the Spirit" listed in Galatians 5, see if you can find at least one or two examples of each quality in Christ's life. Try to avoid any familiar passages that you might automatically turn to; look instead for new examples and insights in the four Gospels.

Love: _____

_____

Joy: _____

_____

Peace: _____

_____

Patience: _____

_____

Kindness: _____

_____

Goodness: _____

_____

Faithfulness: _____

_____

Gentleness: _____

_____

Self-control: _____

_____

🔥 *Living Insights* _____ STUDY TWO

Where is the battle between the flesh and the Spirit the most intense for you? In what ways, specifically?

_____

_____

_____

_____

_____

What effect is it having on your relationship with the Lord and others closest to you?

The Lord

_____

_____

_____

My Closest Friend(s) and Family

_____

_____

_____

So often we get embroiled in conflicts and forget that we have an invincible ally on our side. Have you forgotten? What is it that you could ask His help with at this time? Ask Him. Then pause and set your mind on those things of the Spirit that could bring healing to your relationship with the Lord and your family or best friend. Use the space provided to write down what He brings to mind.

_____

_____

_____

_____

_____

Chapter 4

IS THE SPIRIT'S FILLING THAT BIG A DEAL?

Selected Scriptures

> Do you not know that your body is a temple of the
> Holy Spirit who is in you, whom you have from God,
> and that you are not your own? For you have been
> bought with a price: therefore glorify God in your
> body. (1 Cor. 6:19–20)

The results of the Holy Spirit filling us are nothing short of
remarkable. Our bodies, for example, become temples. Now
don't just whiz by that truth as if you were on board a sight-seeing
bus. Stop and consider this marvel, which all the wonders of the
world combined cannot equal.

At the moment of spiritual rebirth, our bodies become a sacred
sanctuary for the Spirit of the living God. Think about that! Beneath the facade of our flesh and blood dwells the purity, power,
and perfection of the One who created and controls the universe.
He has transformed the frail dust of our humanity into holy ground
for Himself. Even the most venerated cathedrals, with all their
statues and stained glass, are nothing but empty shells in comparison
to the grand glory of one Spirit-filled Christian.

Isn't it staggering to think that we are a living tabernacle for
God's Spirit? Nothing could be more intimate—or more hum-
bling—than the miraculous truth of His holy presence within our
sinful humanity. But thank God He's there. For only He has the
power to cleanse the money-changing attitudes from the inner sanc-
tum of our hearts. Only He can bring about the Christlike beauty
we saw reflected in the things of the Spirit in Galatians 5:22–23.

This is but one facet of what happens when the Spirit fills us. Would
you like to discover more? Then let's begin by examining what the
rest of our opening verse, 1 Corinthians 6:19–20, has to teach us.

A Necessary Reminder of Who—and Whose—We Are

Moving on, the apostle Paul next reminds us that when the
Spirit fills us, *we no longer belong to ourselves but to Christ.* Jesus

redeemed us from our bondage to sin and death with the price of His own blood (see Heb. 9:12–14, 22; 1 Pet. 1:18–19). So as Christians, we belong to Him. He is our new Master. His will has rightful priority over our own selfish desires, and the Holy Spirit "bears witness with our spirit" that we are His (see Rom. 8:16).

The last important result of the Spirit's filling is tucked away in the last half of 1 Corinthians 6:20: *As Christians, we are to glorify Christ.* Notice that Paul doesn't suggest we glorify God when we feel like it or when it is convenient. We are charged to fulfill this responsibility at all times and in every place.

As we saw in our last chapter, however, every believer is burdened with a sin nature that constantly works against our desire to glorify God. That is why we need the Holy Spirit's help, not only for the conviction and faith to be saved, but also for the power to carry out Paul's command to honor God in all that we say and do.

An Essential Revelation of What We Have

The wonderful news of Scripture is that all believers are filled with the Holy Spirit at conversion (see Eph. 1:13–14). He is the fuel, if you will, that empowers our Christian living. But does that mean, then, that we can run out of the Holy Spirit like a car runs out of gas? To find the answer and a deeper understanding of what it means to be filled with the Spirit, let's turn to Ephesians 5.

Therefore be imitators of God, as beloved children; and walk in love, just as Christ also loved you, and gave Himself up for us, an offering and a sacrifice to God as a fragrant aroma. (vv. 1–2)

The wording is different, but the Apostle's aim here is the same as it was in 1 Corinthians 6:20. He wants the Ephesians to glorify the Lord in everything they do, and he communicates this by exhorting them to "walk in love." A little later, in Ephesians 5:8, he reemphasizes the goal, saying, "Walk as children of light." And finally, in verse 15 he writes,

Therefore be careful how you walk, not as unwise men, but as wise, making the most of your time, because the days are evil. So then do not be foolish, but understand what the will of the Lord is. (vv. 15–17)

It takes more than just encouragement and instruction, however, for us to glorify God in our walks as Christians. We need power, and that can only come from following Paul's command in verse 18.

> And do not get drunk with wine, for that is dissipation, but be filled with the Spirit.

Look carefully and you'll recognize that two commands are actually given in this verse. The first is negative: "Do not get drunk with wine." And the second is positive: "Be filled with the Spirit." Now some have mistakenly concluded from this verse that the fullness of the Spirit is like being intoxicated, a sort of spiritual inebriation that leaves you virtually out of control. The problem with this view, of course, is that Paul is not comparing, he's contrasting being filled with the Spirit to being filled with alcohol. In his book *Baptism and Fullness*, John Stott helps us see the contrast more clearly.

> We can indeed agree that in both drunkenness and the fullness of the Spirit two strong influences are at work within us, alcohol in the bloodstream and the Holy Spirit in our hearts. But, whereas excessive alcohol leads to unrestrained and irrational licence, transforming the drunkard into an animal, the fullness of the Spirit leads to restrained and rational moral behaviour, transforming the Christian into the image of Christ. Thus, the results of being under the influence of spirits on the one hand and of the Holy Spirit of God on the other are totally and utterly different. One makes us like beasts, the other like Christ.[1]

With that issue clarified, let's examine the verb "be filled" under John Stott's grammatical microscope to make four telling observations.

> First, it is in the *imperative* mood. "Be filled" is not a tentative suggestion, a mild recommendation, a polite piece of advice. It is a command which comes to us from Christ with all the authority of one of his chosen apostles. We have no more liberty to escape this duty than we have the ethical duties which surround the text, *e.g.* to speak the truth, to

1. John R. W. Stott, *Baptism and Fullness: The Work of the Holy Spirit Today*, 2d ed. (Downers Grove, Ill.: InterVarsity Press, 1979), p. 57.

do honest work, to be kind and forgiving to one another, or to live lives of purity and love. The fullness of the Holy Spirit is not optional for the Christian, but obligatory.

Secondly, the verb is in the *plural* form. So is the preceding verb "do not get drunk with wine". Both imperatives in Ephesians 5:18, the prohibition and the command, are written to the whole Christian community. They are universal in their application. We are none of us to get drunk; we are all of us to be Spirit-filled. The fullness of the Holy Spirit is emphatically not a privilege reserved for some, but a duty resting upon all. . . .

Thirdly, the verb is in the *passive* voice: "be filled". That is, "let the Holy Spirit fill you" (NEB). An important condition of enjoying his fullness is to yield to him without reserve. . . .

Fourthly, the verb is in the *present* tense. It is well known that, in the Greek language, if the imperative is aorist it refers to a single action, while if it is present the action is continuous. Thus, when at the wedding in Cana Jesus said, "fill the jars with water" (Jn. 2:7), the aorist imperative shows that he meant them to do it once only. The present imperative "be filled with the Spirit", on the other hand, indicates not some dramatic or decisive experience which will settle the issue for good, but a continuous appropriation.[2]

Combined, these four points provide a better understanding of what it means to be filled. But the question still remains of what happens when we do yield to Him without reserve. Paul tells us in verses 19–21 of Ephesians 5.

> Speaking to one another in psalms and hymns and spiritual songs, singing and making melody with your heart to the Lord; always giving thanks for all things in the name of our Lord Jesus Christ to God, even the Father; and be subject to one another in the fear of Christ.

2. Stott, *Baptism and Fullness*, pp. 60–61.

Let's listen to Stott again as he draws out four specific results from these verses.

> . . . The first evidence of being filled with the Spirit is that we speak to each other. . . . However deep and intimate our communion with God may seem, we cannot claim the fullness of the Spirit if we are not on speaking terms with any of our fellows. The first sign of fullness is fellowship. . . .
>
> . . . The second result of the Spirit's fullness . . . is "singing and making melody" to the Lord. The Holy Spirit loves to glorify the Lord Jesus, manifesting him to his people in such a way that they delight to sing his praises. . . . The apostle exhorts us not to silent, but to heartfelt, worship.
>
> Thirdly, we are to be "always and for everything giving thanks". Most of us give thanks sometimes for some things; Spirit-filled believers give thanks always for all things. There is not time at which, and no circumstance for which, they do not give thanks. . . . Whenever we start moaning and groaning, it is proof positive that we are not filled with the Spirit. . . .
>
> We have seen that the second and the third marks of the Spirit's fullness are both Godward— singing to the Lord and giving thanks to the Father. . . . The first and fourth marks, however, concern our relationship with each other, speaking to one another and now submitting to one another.
>
> Although the apostle goes on to show that submission is the *particular* duty of a wife to her husband, children to their parents and servants to their masters, he begins by making it the *general* duty of all Christians to each other (which includes husbands, parents and masters). Humble submission is such an important part of Christian behaviour that the verb occurs thirty-two times in the New Testament. Not self-assertion but self-submission is the hall-mark of the Spirit-filled Christian.[3]

3. Stott, *Baptism and Fullness*, pp. 57–59.

A Practical Response to How We Live

No one can say exactly how the Spirit will impact each of our lives. Some results are universal, such as the ones we've seen in this chapter; but the Spirit also transforms each of us uniquely. So it becomes important that we don't compare ourselves with one another or judge the spirituality of another based on our personal experience. With that in mind, here are three helpful comments to remember.

First, for those of you who have not received any exceptional manifestation of the Spirit, remember that such experiences are not necessary for Christian maturity. Some have them, yes, but let's not be worried or afraid we're missing something just because He hasn't manifested Himself in the same way with us.

Second, for those of you who have experienced something far more dynamic and expressive from the Spirit, remember that what God has given you may not be for everyone. Try hard not to stereotype the Spirit's work to always match what He's done for you.

Third, for all Christians, let us seek ways to enjoy our vast common ground rather than splinter into defensive groups. Allow Paul's words in Ephesians 4 to linger long enough in your mind so that they become your way of life—the way of life the Spirit wants you to be filled with.

> I, therefore, the prisoner of the Lord, entreat you to walk in a manner worthy of the calling with which you have been called, with all humility and gentleness, with patience, showing forbearance to one another in love, being diligent to preserve the unity of the Spirit in the bond of peace. (vv. 1–3)

 Living Insights STUDY ONE

I don't know about you, but I can't get over this idea that my body is a temple for the Holy Spirit—God's Spirit, the pillar of fire, the burning bush, the thunder and smoke of Sinai! Whoa, that's exciting! Now, of course, I don't expect a cloud to descend upon me with fearsome bolts of lightning scaring the pants off all my friends, but it is downright thrilling to think that this gimp-kneed temple of mine is filled with such an awesome Presence.

Sure, I've known this truth about the Holy Spirit for years. Probably you have too. But it was never more to me than just another piece of the pneumatological puzzle I learned to put together in seminary. This whole concept is so new to me, really, that I've only now begun to grasp some of its fantastic meaning.

Have you really ever thought much about your body being His temple? Has anyone ever helped you appreciate all that it means? It is truly transforming, able to change the way we look at ourselves, our worth, our competence, our sense of belonging. The tragedy, of course, is that so many of us have completely missed it.

If you've never considered this truth as anything more than just the stuff of dry doctrine, would you set aside the rest of this day, this week, to think about all the ramifications of what it means to have the Spirit living in you? How does this truth affect the way you view yourself? Does it change the way you live? Does it make your relationship with the Lord a more personal one?

Just for fun, you might even ask your friends about this. See if they have ever caught hold of the perspective that they are walking temples of the living Spirit of God. We'll provide space to journal your thoughts as you and the Holy Spirit draw closer together over this incredible truth.

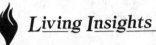

Uh-oh. Putt putt, sputter, wheeeeeze. Your spiritual tank just hit empty. You've been running on fumes for the last day or so, and now you're completely out. No more coasting. Either you pull over and be filled with the Spirit, or you'll just have to leave your spiritual life stranded where it is and buzz on down the road without it. What are you going to do?

It's amazing how many of us just keep right on going. I'm guilty of it. And I'm sure you've done the same thing a time or two yourself. Sure, we'll stop whenever our cars need fuel. In fact, we'll often stop for a refill when the tank is only half or three-quarters empty. But stop whenever our Christian walk needs a fresh filling of the Holy Spirit? Naaah. Too much trouble, too inconvenient right now. We can make it a little bit further, we think. But you and I both know what happens when a person doesn't stay filled with the Spirit.

Frankly, a lot of us are coasting in the Christian community; a lot of us are getting stranded and deciding just to leave our Christian commitment where it sits and walk away. Then, too, there are a lot of us who, instead of refilling our spiritual tank, are straining in the strength of our own flesh to push our spirituality everywhere we want it to go.

So what are you going to do? If you choose to be filled again with the Spirit as the apostle Paul commands us in Ephesians 5:18, then take a moment to read and follow these helpful instructions from J. Dwight Pentecost's book *The Divine Comforter*.

> Until an individual voluntarily submits to control by the Spirit of God, he will not be filled and controlled by the Spirit. This gives importance to such passages of Scripture as, "I beseech you therefore, brethren, by the mercies of God, *that ye present* your bodies a living sacrifice, holy, acceptable unto God, which is your reasonable service" (Romans 12:1). The words "that ye present" refer to the act . . . in which one disclaims ownership of himself, discounts all rights to himself, and acknowledges God's ownership and God's right to him as a person.

This same truth is presented when Paul says, ". . . yield yourselves unto God . . ." (Romans 6:13). . . . That act is the presenting or yielding necessary for the filling of the Spirit. There are many of God's children who have never experienced the fullness of the Holy Spirit in their lives, day by day, because they never have come to the place where they are willing to surrender their own wills, their own way, their own wisdom, their own goals, ambitions and desires, to say, "Lord, I am stepping down off the throne of my life, and from this moment on I am acknowledging Your right to my life, to take it and use it as You see fit."[4]

That's the price of the Spirit's filling. Are you willing to pay?

4. J. Dwight Pentecost, *The Divine Comforter: The Person and Work of the Holy Spirit* (reprint; 1963, Chicago, Ill.: Moody Press, 1975), pp. 159–61.

Chapter 5

THE SPIRIT WHO SURPRISES

1 Corinthians 2:1–13

In his book *It Was on Fire When I Lay Down on It*, Robert Fulghum recalls a wonderful story from his fatherhood days that warms the heart with an unforgettable lesson.

The cardboard box is marked "the good stuff."

. . .

One of the keepsakes in the box is a small paper bag. Lunch size. Though the top is sealed with duct tape, staples, and several paper clips, there is a ragged rip in one side through which the contents may be seen.

This particular lunch sack has been in my care for maybe fourteen years. But it really belongs to my daughter, Molly. Soon after she came of school age, she became an enthusiastic participant in packing the morning lunches for herself, her brothers, and me. Each bag got a share of sandwiches, apples, milk money, and sometimes a note or a treat. One morning Molly handed me two bags as I was about to leave. One regular lunch sack. And the one with the duct tape and staples and paper clips. "Why two bags?" "The other one is something else." "What's in it?" "Just some stuff—take it with you." Not wanting to hold court over the matter, I stuffed both sacks into my briefcase, kissed the child, and rushed off.

At midday, while hurriedly scarfing down my real lunch, I tore open Molly's bag and shook out the contents. Two hair ribbons, three small stones, a plastic dinosaur, a pencil stub, a tiny seashell, two animal crackers, a marble, a used lipstick, a small doll, two chocolate kisses, and thirteen pennies.

I smiled. How charming. Rising to hustle off to all the important business of the afternoon, I swept the desk clean—into the wastebasket—leftover lunch,

Molly's junk, and all. There wasn't anything in there I needed.

That evening Molly came to stand beside me while I was reading the paper. "Where's my bag?" "What bag?" "You know, the one I gave you this morning." "I left it at the office, why?" "I forgot to put this note in it." She hands over the note. "Besides, I want it back." "Why?" "Those are my things in the sack, Daddy, the ones I really like—I thought you might like to play with them, but now I want them back. You didn't lose the bag, did you, Daddy?" Tears puddled in her eyes. "Oh no, I just forgot to bring it home," I lied. "Bring it tomorrow, okay?" "Sure thing—don't worry." As she hugged my neck with relief, I unfolded the note that had not got into the sack: "I love you, Daddy."

Oh.

And also—uh-oh.

I looked long at the face of my child.

She was right—what was in that sack was "something else."

Molly had given me her treasures. All that a seven-year-old held dear. Love in a paper sack. And I had missed it. Not only missed it, but had thrown it in the wastebasket because "there wasn't anything in there I needed." Dear God.

It wasn't the first or the last time I felt my Daddy Permit was about to run out.

It was a long trip back to the office. But there was nothing else to be done. So I went. The pilgrimage of a penitent. Just ahead of the janitor, I picked up the wastebasket and poured the contents on my desk. . . .

After washing the mustard off the dinosaurs and spraying the whole thing with breath-freshener to kill the smell of onions, I carefully smoothed out the wadded ball of brown paper into a semifunctional bag and put the treasures inside and carried the whole thing home gingerly, like an injured kitten. The next evening I returned it to Molly, no questions asked, no explanations offered. The bag didn't look so good, but the stuff was all there and that's what counted. . . .

To my surprise, Molly gave the bag to me once again several days later. Same ratty bag. Same stuff inside. I felt forgiven. And trusted. And loved. And a little more comfortable wearing the title of Father. Over several months the bag went with me from time to time. It was never clear to me why I did or did not get it on a given day. I began to think of it as the Daddy Prize and tried to be good the night before so I might be given it the next morning.

In time Molly turned her attention to other things . . . found other treasures . . . lost interest in the game . . . grew up. Something. Me? I was left holding the bag. She gave it to me one morning and never asked for its return. And so I have it still. . . .

So the worn paper sack is there in the box. Left over from a time when a child said, "Here—this is the best I've got. Take it—it's yours. Such as I have, give I to thee."

I missed it the first time. But it's my bag now.[1]

The priceless treasures of a father's little girl. Love in a paper sack. Think of what Fulghum almost missed, did miss, but then recovered. What a gift!

As Christians, we, too, have been given a gift, a priceless treasure from our heavenly Father. All that He holds dear He has entrusted to each of us. Not love in a paper sack, but in a Person—His Spirit. And we've missed it. Not only missed it, but many have mentally swept His work of searching, teaching, and revealing into the wastebasket of forgetfulness simply because it didn't seem all that important, practical or necessary. Dear God.

If this has happened to you, then come with us on a pilgrimage of the penitent to the Upper Room and rediscover the treasure Jesus gave when He said to the disciples, "Here—this is the best I've got. Take Him—He's yours. Such as I have, give I to thee."

1. Robert Fulghum, *It Was on Fire When I Lay Down on It* (New York, N.Y.: Villard Books, 1989), pp. 27–31.

A Reminder of What Jesus Promised

Jesus promised that He would

> "ask the Father, and He will give you another Helper, that He may be with you forever; that is the Spirit of truth, whom the world cannot receive, because it does not behold Him or know Him, but you know Him because He abides with you, and will be in you. I will not leave you as orphans. . . . The Helper, the Holy Spirit, whom the Father will send in My name, He will teach you all things, and bring to your remembrance all that I said to you." (John 14:16–18a, 26)

Let's spend some time getting to know our Helper.

The Meaning of the Spirit's Name: "Helper"

The Greek term for "Helper" is made up of *para*, which means "alongside something," and *kaleō*, which means "to call out." Combined they describe the Spirit as One called alongside to help. In what way He'll help, exactly, is revealed in the latter half of verse 26. First, He will teach us all things. And second, He will guide our memories to recall all that Jesus has said.

An Often-Overlooked Ministry of the Spirit

Later that same evening, Jesus explained still more specifics about the Spirit's unique role as our Helper.

> "I tell you the truth, it is to your advantage that I go away; for if I do not go away, the Helper shall not come to you; but if I go, I will send Him to you. And He, when He comes, will convict the world concerning sin, and righteousness, and judgment; concerning sin, because they do not believe in Me; and concerning righteousness, because I go to the Father, and you no longer behold Me; and concerning judgment, because the ruler of this world has been judged. I have many more things to say to you, but you cannot bear them now. But when He, the Spirit of truth, comes, He will guide you into all the truth; for He will not speak on His own initiative, but whatever He hears, He will speak; and He will disclose to you what is to come. He shall glorify Me;

for He shall take of Mine, and shall disclose it to you. All things that the Father has are Mine; therefore I said, that He takes of Mine, and will disclose it to you." (16:7–15)

Notice in particular what Christ predicts about the Spirit in verse 13. He will help clarify the truth and disclose things once known only between the Father and the Son. And the exciting news is that the Helper is still carrying out those same two functions today! He's still in the business of illuminating the Scriptures, giving us understanding, helping us discern truth from error.

All of us can probably point to some specific moments in our lives when we experienced the Spirit's unmistakable guidance. Why, though, is our awareness of the Spirit's work and our sense of intimacy with Him so often lacking? Perhaps because we have never really studied or understood the Helper's inner workings.

Some Examples of the Spirit's Inner Workings

Fortunately, we can gain a deeper awareness of the Spirit through the apostle Paul's first letter to the Corinthians. Through the transparency of his writing in chapter 2, we can trace the inner workings of the Helper that continue in our lives as well.

Demonstrating God's Unique Power

First Corinthians 2 opens with a clear statement not only about Paul's ministry but also about the Holy Spirit's. The two are blended together in the first five verses, telling us (1) what Paul didn't do, (2) what he did do, and (3) how the Apostle accomplished what he did.

> And when I came to you, brethren, I did not come with superiority of speech or of wisdom, proclaiming to you the testimony of God. For I determined to know nothing among you except Jesus Christ, and Him crucified. And I was with you in weakness and in fear and in much trembling. And my message and my preaching were not in persuasive words of wisdom, but in demonstration of the Spirit and of power, that your faith should not rest on the wisdom of men, but on the power of God. (vv. 1–5)

To the surprise of many, Paul did not come to Corinth as a

41

fast-talking ringmaster with a show-stopping message from God. Instead, he proved to be a very ordinary, somewhat disappointing figure of a leader who monotonously preached the same basic message. So how did he accomplish the miraculous results of bringing others to Christ and establishing a vibrant church in Corinth? By the *dunamis* of the Holy Spirit (vv. 4–5)! The Helper empowered Paul's message and his ministry in that community. The inner working of the Spirit was evident to all by the presence of a power that could not be defined, duplicated, or, most importantly, denied.

Searching God's Hidden Wisdom

As we read in verse 4, Paul reminds the Corinthians that his preaching was "not in persuasive words of wisdom." But that's not to say it lacked any wisdom at all. On the contrary, he writes,

> We do speak wisdom among those who are mature; a wisdom, however, not of this age, nor of the rulers of this age, who are passing away; but we speak God's wisdom in a mystery, the hidden wisdom, which God predestined before the ages to our glory; the wisdom which none of the rulers of this age has understood; for if they had understood it, they would not have crucified the Lord of glory; but just as it is written,
>
> > "Things which eye has not seen and ear has
> > not heard,
> > And which have not entered the heart of
> > man,
> > All that God has prepared for those who love
> > Him."
>
> For to us God revealed them through the Spirit; for the Spirit searches all things, even the depths of God. (vv. 6–10)

The wisdom Paul preached was not taught to him by any ruler from any age of this world. His wisdom came from the Spirit, who dives into the depths of God to bring us His hidden treasures of truth. Without the Spirit's help, the deep wealth of God would forever be out of our reach.

> Oh, the depth of the riches both of the wisdom

and knowledge of God! How unsearchable are His judgments and unfathomable His ways! For who has known the mind of the Lord, or who became His counselor? Or who has first given to Him that it might be paid back to him again? For from Him and through Him and to Him are all things. To Him be the glory forever. Amen. (Rom. 11:33–35)

What we could not do in our weakness, God accomplishes for us through His Spirit.

Revealing God's Deep Thoughts

For who among men knows the thoughts of a man except the spirit of the man, which is in him? Even so the thoughts of God no one knows except the Spirit of God. Now we have received, not the spirit of the world, but the Spirit who is from God, that we might know the things freely given to us by God. (1 Cor. 2:11–12)

None of us could comprehend the thoughts of God without His Spirit revealing them to us also. "For," as the Lord reminds us in Isaiah,

"My thoughts are not your thoughts,
Neither are your ways My ways," declares the
Lord.
"For as the heavens are higher than the earth,
So are My ways higher than your ways,
And My thoughts than your thoughts."
(Isa. 55:8–9)

Bridging the chasm so that we might have an inner wisdom and assurance the world does not have is the Holy Spirit. His ministry of revealing "the things freely given to us by God" may very well explain how you or I can have a confidence in a certain matter that others may not share. "Haven't you had that happen?" asks Chuck Swindoll.

You have pored over something in prayer, waited on God, searched His truths in the Scriptures, and then come to a settled conviction: "This is what I ought to do." Or perhaps, "This is what I ought not to do."

Others don't agree with you. Others around you cannot see the logic of it. Yet it is as though you are
"bound in the Spirit" to carry out your conviction
because you know it is what God would have you do.
It may seem surprising to some and stupid to others,
but you know it's what you must do. The longer I
live, the more I believe that that kind of wisdom,
conviction, knowledge is the work of the Spirit.[2]

Teaching God's Profound Insights

Which things we also speak, not in words taught by
human wisdom, but in those taught by the Spirit,
combining spiritual thoughts with spiritual words.
(1 Cor. 2:13)

Following His ministry of searching God's wisdom and revealing
it to Paul, the Spirit imparted to him the very words needed to
share the spiritual treasures he had been given. The Apostle continually combined spiritual thoughts with spiritual words, cultivat-
ing in himself the "mind of Christ" (v. 16).

That same Helper who searched, taught, and revealed God's
wisdom and power to Paul is at work in you and me today. In place
of weakness, He brings strength. In place of human knowledge, He
brings divine wisdom. In place of superficial understanding, He
brings profound insights. He's constantly at work on your behalf.
He is your treasure. All that the Lord of this universe holds dear
He has entrusted to you. "Here—this is the best I've got. Take
Him—He's yours. Such as I have, give I to thee."

You may have missed this incredible gift before. Do you see Him
now?

 Living Insights

I have a suspicion that many of us miss seeing the Spirit's work
in our lives, not because we must be mystics to perceive His help,
but because we're unfamiliar with His ministry as it is defined in
the Scriptures.

---

2. Charles R. Swindoll, *Flying Closer to the Flame* (Dallas, Tex.: Word Books, Publisher, 1993),
chap. 5.

When a specific biblical principle comes to mind in the very moment we need it, for example, do we recognize that as the Spirit doing His work of revealing, or do we simply chalk that up to our intuition or just plain dumb luck? Or how about when we're studying the Scriptures and a passage opens up and our thinking is impacted to a depth of understanding we've never known before? Is that superior intelligence or is it the Holy Spirit helping us search God's wisdom, teaching us profound insights?

Some of us don't even bother to credit anybody or anything for these things. They just happen and we go on. But think of what we're missing! The Spirit is right there, He's just tapped us on the shoulder, but we hurry right past Him as if He didn't exist. And then we complain to others about how distant the Spirit feels to us. True, He is like the wind, but even a schoolboy can recognize the wind's effect when he sees it. In the same way, we can learn to better recognize the Spirit's work when we see it.

Your assignment, if you will, is to look closely this next week for evidences of the Spirit's presence in your life. Now we could easily fall into error with this if not guided by the Scriptures. So I want you to specifically watch for His movement in three of the four areas identified from the Scriptures in the chapter. For example, *demonstrating God's unique power*. Have you seen the dynamic of the Spirit working in people's lives lately? A conversion, perhaps, or a dead church coming to life through revival, or the transformation of an individual's character from darkness to light?

Under each example of the Spirit's inner workings, keep a record of the sightings you make. And don't be surprised if He taps you on the shoulder a time or two as well!

Demonstrating God's Unique Power

_____

_____

_____

Revealing God's Deep Thoughts

_____

_____

_____

_____

_____

_____

Living Insights

Let's just imagine for a moment what the world would be like without the Spirit. First read John 16:8–11 and then write a brief description in the space provided.

_____

_____

_____

_____

On a more personal level now, imagine what you would be like without the Spirit. You're a Christian, but what would life be like if the Helper hadn't come? What are some of the consequences and hardships you would face? Give this some thought, and then write down as detailed an answer as you can. (Seeking the Spirit's help in answering the question is permitted!)

_____

_____

_____

_____

_____

Why all this imagining life without the Spirit? Because perhaps it will help some of you gain a fresh perspective on His importance and influence. Perhaps it will enable you, with the Holy Spirit's help of course, to recognize and appreciate more of what He's doing in your own life.

Chapter 6

DRAW ME NEARER...
NEARER

Selected Scriptures

Baptists, Methodists, Presbyterians—whatever the denomination, Christians everywhere are intrigued by the Holy Spirit. Like the proverbial moth and flame, however, we don't know how close we can fly without burning our wings. We are attracted by the light, but at the same time, we are frightened by the heat.

A Candid Confession That Concerns Us

Have you ever felt a pull to draw closer to the Holy Spirit, only to have it blocked because of fear? Fear of being misunderstood and mislabeled. Fear of going off the emotional deep end and getting weird. Fear of falling away from Scripture into error.

Why is that? Why are so many of us afraid of the Holy Spirit? Could it be because we have bought into the view that the spiritual world is flat and that if we sail too close to the edge exploring the Holy Spirit we just might fall off?[1]

It may sound ridiculous, but deep down that's exactly the fear some of us have. We believe the frightening tales others have told about those who have dared to sail beyond the charted edges of our limited understanding. So instead of venturing out, we drop anchor in the shallow waters of theoretical knowledge and gather barnacles.

Still, the wind blows, and from time to time we feel the urge to cast off our fear and head for deeper waters. We sense the need to unfurl our sails and follow the Spirit's filling as He navigates us into all truth. We were made for such adventure. We're about to begin one now.

So come aboard, if you've the heart for it, and let's push off to explore a new horizon of the Holy Spirit.

A Closer Examination That Enlightens Us

To begin our journey, we must first pass through some familiar

---

1. Some of the thoughts and questions in this chapter have been adapted from a personal letter to Chuck Swindoll dated July 31, 1992.

waters in Ephesians 5. As you may recall, the apostle Paul exhorted believers to walk in a manner that glorifies the Lord (vv. 2, 8, 15). In addition, he also issued several warnings: Don't be immoral, impure, or greedy (v. 3); don't lose control of your tongue (v. 4); don't be deceived (v. 6); don't participate in evil deeds of darkness (v. 11); don't be unwise (v. 15); don't be foolish (v. 17); and don't get drunk (v. 18a). As a climax to all those negatives, Paul then put forth one grand positive: *Be filled with the Spirit* (v. 18b). In other words, let Him guide you; follow His directions so that your faith doesn't suffer shipwreck on any of the reefs of unrighteousness Paul pointed out.

Pushing on from Ephesians 5, let's set our course next for Acts 6, where we can explore a little further this idea of being filled with the Spirit.

Because certain needs were being overlooked among the believers in Jerusalem's early church, the Apostles suggested that seven men be selected to serve and meet those needs. As for qualifications, the Twelve recommended that each man have a good reputation, be full of wisdom, and be *full of the Spirit* (v. 3). One of those chosen who clearly met those conditions was a disciple named Stephen (v. 5). He went on to have such a dynamic ministry that not even his adversaries could "cope with the wisdom and the Spirit with which he was speaking" (v. 10).

Frustrated by their inability to intimidate or refute Stephen, his opponents had him arrested on the trumped-up testimony of false witnesses (vv. 11–15). Chapter 7 then records Stephen's remarkable defense before the Sanhedrin, which he concluded with these piercing words:

> "You men who are stiff-necked and uncircumcised in heart and ears are always resisting the Holy Spirit; you are doing just as your fathers did. Which one of the prophets did your fathers not persecute? And they killed those who had previously announced the coming of the Righteous One, whose betrayers and murderers you have now become; you who received the law as ordained by angels, and yet did not keep it."
>
> Now when they heard this, they were cut to the quick, and they began gnashing their teeth at him. But being full of the Holy Spirit, he gazed intently

into heaven and saw the glory of God, and Jesus standing at the right hand of God; and he said, "Behold, I see the heavens opened up and the Son of Man standing at the right hand of God." (vv. 51–56)

In a rather dramatic and obviously supernatural way, Stephen's experience reminds us of some of the truths that we learned in our last chapter. Namely, that we have been given the Holy Spirit so that

(1) "we might know the things freely given to us by God" (1 Cor. 2:12)—Stephen certainly knew;

(2) we might speak the thoughts given to us by God (v. 13)—Stephen spoke;

(3) we might "appraise" all things (v. 15)—Stephen's wise appraisal of the truth far exceeded his accusers'.

In Greek, the term for *appraise* means "to sift, to examine, to decide correctly." The Spirit-filled believer is able to discern and understand truth that the nonbeliever cannot. "Like a deaf critic of Bach or a blind critic of Raphael is the unregenerate critic of God's Word."[2]

Not one of the seventy-one members of the Sanhedrin, Israel's highest religious body, grasped the significance of Stephen's message. Without the Holy Spirit they were deaf to the truth he spoke and blind to the vision he saw.

For another glimpse of the Spirit's gifting to know and discern God's truth, let's put out from Acts and set our course for the "anointing" in 1 John. Our destination is a letter written by the apostle John to Christians whom he endearingly calls his "children" (see 2:1, 12, 18). More particularly, we want to come alongside verses 20 and 27 of chapter 2 to look closely at something special John says we've received from the Lord.

But you have an anointing from the Holy One, and you all know. . . . And as for you, the anointing which you received from Him abides in you, and you have no need for anyone to teach you; but as

---

2. Stanley D. Toussaint, "Acts," in *The Bible Knowledge Commentary*, New Testament ed., ed. John F. Walvoord, Roy B. Zuck (Wheaton, Ill.: Scripture Press Publications, Victor Books, 1983), p. 510.

His anointing teaches you about all things, and is true and is not a lie, and just as it has taught you, you abide in Him. (vv. 20, 27)

Even though these are the only three times in the Apostle's letter that he mentions the idea of anointing, if we look closely with the help of commentator Kenneth Wuest we can uncover several important insights.

First: *What does it mean?* The word for *anointing* is *chrisma*, and it

> refers to that with which the anointing is performed, the unguent or ointment. Here it refers to the Holy Spirit with whom the believer is anointed. The two words meaning "to anoint" in the New Testament, *aleiphō* and *chriō*, refer to the act of applying something to something else for a certain purpose. *Aleiphō* was used, for instance, . . . of the act of greasing the yoke-band of an ox . . . so that it would not irritate the sleek hide of the ox. *Chriō* was used of the application of a lotion to a sick horse. Thus, the anointing with the Holy Spirit refers to the act of God the Father (applying to the believing sinner) sending the Spirit in answer to the prayer of God the Son to take up His permanent residence in the believer.[3]

Second: *How often does it happen?* Over in James 4:5, the Apostle

> refers to the initial coming of the Spirit into the heart of the believing sinner at the moment he places his faith in the Saviour. This anointing is never repeated. The Old Testament priests were anointed with oil just once, when they were inducted into their office. The New Testament priest (the believer) is anointed with the Spirit just once, when he is inducted into his office as a priest (when he is saved).[4]

Third: *How long does it last?* John himself answers this: "As for

3. Kenneth S. Wuest, *In These Last Days: 2 Peter, 1, 2, 3 John, and Jude in the Greek New Testament* (Grand Rapids, Mich.: William B. Eerdmans Publishing Co., 1954), p. 132.
4. Wuest, *In These Last Days*, p. 132.

you, the anointing which you received from Him abides in you" (1 John 2:27). As Wuest explains, this teaches us

> that the Holy Spirit who is that with which the saint is anointed, stays in that person forever. . . . David could pray, "Take not thy Holy Spirit from me" (Psalm 51:11), since the Spirit came upon an individual in Old Testament times for the period of that person's ministry, and left him when that ministry was over, without affecting his salvation. But in New Testament times, the Spirit is in the believer to stay.[5]

Fourth: *What does it provide?*

> One of the ministries of the Spirit consequent upon His indwelling presence is that of enlightening [the Christian] regarding the meaning of the Word of God. He is the Great Teacher in the Church. As a result of this, John says, "Ye know all things" (A.V.). But the word "all" in the best Greek texts is in the nominative case, which makes it the subject of the verb. The correct translation is, "Ye all know." That is, as a result of the indwelling of the Holy Spirit, the saints are given the ability to know God's truth. The particular word for "know" here is not *ginosko*, "to know by experience," but *oida*, "to know absolutely and finally." . . . This ability to know the truth gives the saints the ability also to detect error.[6]

Questions and Observations That Intrigue Us

We've come far in our exploration of the Spirit, so perhaps now is a good time for us to log in our minds some intriguing questions about our journey thus far. Remember, these are not assertions of fact. We're just asking, wondering, probing with wide-eyed, child-like curiosity.

> [1] Would this anointing explain what we commonly call intuition? . . . Are we giving credit to intuition that really belongs to the Holy Spirit?

5. Wuest, *In These Last Days*, pp. 137–138.
6. Wuest, *In These Last Days*, p. 133.

I cannot say for sure, but perhaps we are. . . .

[2] If we are full of the Spirit, can we envision things others cannot? Again, I'm not affirming it, I'm only asking. Since Stephen was able to do so, can any believer? Since the Spirit searches all things, could He give us insight and on-the-spot discernment that transcend human ability, academic learning, and personal training? He's God; why couldn't He?

[3] And if that is true, wouldn't those who oppose us find themselves unable to stand against us . . . unable to "withstand"? I lean toward saying yes. It's what we might call a "supernatural sense of invincibility." And at times I have experienced it, that underlying sense of absolute confidence. Perhaps you have as well. In those moments of unusual courage—without any credit to myself —I am not afraid to stand absolutely alone.

Could that inner confidence be part of the anointing?[7]

A Few Words of Warning

Ken Gire once wrote, "Questions . . . are the grappling hooks by which sheer summits of truth can be scaled."[8] We cannot climb out of our ignorance without them especially as it concerns the Holy Spirit. But we mustn't attempt the climb without observing certain basic safety precautions. Here are a few words of warning to keep you from falling into error.

Hopefully all this won't get kicked sideways in your mind and twist up some awfully good theology. To keep that from happening, let me caution you. . . .

Balance is always preferred to extremes. . . . Stay reasonable, Christian friend. Don't go home and start praying for some middle-of-the-night visions; that's not biblical. Keep a level head. Don't get weird.

7. Charles R. Swindoll, *Flying Closer to the Flame* (Dallas, Tex.: Word Publishing, 1993), chap. 6.

8. From the study guide, *Issues and Answers in Jesus' Day*, coauthored by Ken Gire, from the Bible-teaching ministry of Charles R. Swindoll (Fullerton, Calif.: Insight for Living, 1990), p. 2.

. . . Don't start setting dates for Jesus' return. Don't play with snakes and scorpions. Don't sacrifice your solid biblical roots and orthodox theology on the altar of bizarre experiences. Don't start attending meetings where legs are lengthened and teeth are filled. That kind of sideshow stuff may draw a crowd, but it is not the anointing.

The anointing is a knowledge. You know something.[9]

A Final Suggestion That Frees Us

Don't let fear take the wind out of your sails, leaving you dead in the water of doldrums. Come with us as we journey on into new chapters. Adventure awaits—there is so much more to the Spirit's work within us than many of us have ever known or experienced!

 Living Insights

Instead of being anointed with oil as the kings, priests, and prophets were in Old Testament days, we have been anointed with the Spirit, with a person, with a power, with the divine Comforter Jesus promised.[10] And we know from our study in previous chapters that He has come to fill, transform, teach, and reveal, just to name a few different aspects of His ministry.

In 1 John 2, the Apostle specifically focuses on how the Spirit with whom we have been anointed gives us an ability to discern truth. This was crucial for his readers to remember, because their knowledge was being tested by false teachers whom John calls antichrists (vv. 18–22). It wasn't that the Apostle was telling them they needed new spiritual insight or knowledge; rather, as William Barclay writes,

> John is pleading with his people to abide in the things which they have learned, for, if they do, they will abide in Christ. . . .

9. Swindoll, *Flame*, chap. 6.

10. Examples of anointing in the Old Testament are found in Exodus 28:41; 40:13–15; 1 Samuel 10:1; 16:12–13; 1 Kings 1:39 and 19:16.

. . . Westcott puts it in this way: "The object of the apostle in writing was not to communicate fresh knowledge, but to bring into active and decisive use the knowledge which his readers already possessed." The greatest Christian defence is simply to remember what we know. What we need is not new truth, but that the truth which we already know become active and effective in our lives.[11]

Are you being challenged right now about truth you already know? Perhaps by a professor in a philosophy class, the playboy attitude of a coworker, or the heretical teachings of someone within the church? What you need, probably, is not some new revelation to deal with this; rather, you need the Spirit's assistance in recalling and correctly applying the truth He's already taught you. Remember, He reveals the things given to us by God, and He teaches us to combine spiritual thoughts with spiritual words (1 Cor. 2:12–13).

Pause now for prayer, and ask the Spirit to bring to mind any truths that might apply in your particular situation. Then listen . . . and keep listening. It could be that He will bring a specific passage to mind right away, or perhaps tomorrow or the next day. Or it could be that He may use a close friend to remind you of some relevant Scriptures. Really, it's impossible to say exactly how or when the Spirit will work. The point is, keep seeking and trusting. He is there and He does want to give you the wisdom you need. Have the faith to trust Him for His help.

Use the space provided to jot down any thoughts and passages of Scripture that come to mind. In the end, it will be an exciting record of the Spirit's involvement with you in this situation.

_____

_____

_____

_____

_____

_____

11. William Barclay, *The Letters of John and Jude*, rev. ed., The Daily Study Bible Series (Philadelphia, Pa.: Westminster Press, 1976), pp. 69, 66.

_____

_____

_____

_____

_____

 ## Living Insights

Thus far we've seen the Spirit do some pretty amazing things. For example, we saw how He miraculously emboldened the disciples to preach "with other tongues" to a mixed multitude on the day of Pentecost (Acts 2). We saw Him use Peter and John to heal a lame man and demonstrate a confidence in court that confounded their accusers (chaps. 3–4). And we've seen Him empower Stephen to perform "great wonders and signs" as well as receive an incredible glimpse into heaven (chaps. 6–7).

All of this, combined with the exciting results He brings about when He fills us, is wonderful to see about the Holy Spirit. But it's also easy to misconstrue so that we end up thinking that the "victorious life must be very exciting—a supernatural life, a living miracle, a thrilling adventure demonstrating God's power. . . ."[12] But as Dr. Charles Trumbull points out,

> Right there lies [a] peril—to mistakenly expect thrilling, unexpected, supernatural evidences of God's power. And if these phenomena do not occur, we are tempted to think something is wrong. God wants us to trust, not in supernatural experiences, but in Himself. He will decide when the unusual shall come into our life, and when our life shall be commonplace and humdrum, so far as things of sight and sense are concerned. It is safe to say that God's purpose for the supernatural, so far as circumstances and experience are concerned, is the unusual rather

12. Leona Frances Choy, _Powerlines: What Great Evangelicals Believed about the Holy Spirit 1850–1930_ (Camp Hill, Pa.: Christian Publications, 1990), p. 309.

than the usual for His wholly trusting children. Don't test God or your victory by circumstances or manifestations. Trust only Jesus Himself.[13]

A little further on, Trumbull adds this practical caution:

The blessings of God in this life in the Spirit are so wonderful that we are in danger of thinking more about the blessings than of the Blesser. God does not want us to worship the fruit or gifts of the Spirit, but the Spirit.[14]

So often in Christian circles, the Holy Spirit has been reduced to nothing more than a genie in a lamp. He's treated as a cosmic bellboy ready to fulfill our every whim or expectation. We peddle Him and His power like a cheap sideshow: "Come one, come all to the greatest show on earth. See the Holy Spirit perform death-defying healings and other miraculous feats of signs and wonders."

I mention all this just as a word of caution, something to help keep you on course in our journey of discovery about the Holy Spirit. It's appropriate for all of us to check our focus now as we near the halfway mark in our study. Keep your eyes, as Trumbull says, on the Blesser and not the blessings, and you'll steer clear of these perils and sail on into a solid relationship with the Lord.

13. Charles Gallaudet Trumbull, "Don't Paddle Your Own Canoe," in Powerlines, by Leona Frances Choy, p. 309.

14. Trumbull, "Don't Paddle Your Own Canoe," p. 310.

Chapter 7

THOSE UNIDENTIFIED INNER PROMPTINGS

Selected Scriptures

Hurry! Buckle up. The countdown has already begun.
Five . . . four . . . three . . . two . . . one . . . ignition
—blast-off! We have lift-off. All systems are go. We're off on another
intriguing journey of discovery about the Holy Spirit. Where are we
going, you say? Why, space, of course. No, no, no, not outer space,
inner space—the heart, mind, and soul. You know, that mysterious
realm where the Spirit lives and works. Our mission is to explore the
existence of UIPs—unidentified inner promptings. For example, is
it possible that some UIPs are actually the Holy Spirit working in
the ways we studied in chapter 5? Could it be that what we call
intuition is, at times, the guiding and convicting effect of the Spirit?

Probing to find answers to questions like this won't be easy, but
it is important. For in striving to avoid reading the Spirit into every
whim that crosses our minds, many of us have made the opposite
mistake of throwing the baby out with the bath water. We've limited
our contact with Him to only impersonal doctrinal discussions. But
surely if we are sensitive to God's Word and ways, there will be
those undeniable brushes with the Spirit when we feel His divine
guidance and conviction.

Exploring the Spirit's unidentified inner promptings pushes us
beyond the comfortable limits of precise knowledge to the edge of
mystery in the Christian experience. The mystery is that we never
know when, where, or how, exactly, the Spirit will touch our lives. No
one will ever resolve that riddle, and certainly that is not our aim here.
Rather, our goal is to heighten our awareness of the Person behind
some of the mystery so that we give Him the credit He deserves, instead of chalking things up to luck, coincidence, or intuition. Perhaps
then we will have made a significant discovery and a more personal
connection with the Holy Spirit who strives within on our behalf.

We Are Fearfully and Wonderfully Made

Some of us have been asleep about the Spirit's work in our lives for so long that we need a wake-up call, and Psalm 139 is a rousing place to start in reaffirming some basic truths. David asks,

> Where can I go from Thy Spirit?
> Or where can I flee from Thy presence? (v. 7)

The implied answer in the eloquent verses that follow is an emphatic *nowhere!*

> If I ascend to heaven, Thou art there;
> If I make my bed in Sheol, behold, Thou art there.
> If I take the wings of the dawn,
> If I dwell in the remotest part of the sea,
> Even there Thy hand will lead me,
> And Thy right hand will lay hold of me.
> (vv. 8–10)

Taking the broad truth of the Spirit's inescapable presence even further, David next focuses on the craftsmanship of the Creator inside a mother's womb.

> For Thou didst form my inward parts;
> Thou didst weave me in my mother's womb.
> I will give thanks to Thee, for I am fearfully and
>   wonderfully made;
> Wonderful are Thy works,
> And my soul knows it very well. (vv. 13–14)

> Caught up in the wonder of it all, the ancient writer exclaims how uniquely created we are. I suggest that uniqueness includes secret inner chambers and hidden capacities other created beings lack. I also would suggest that such an inner system provides for the reception of divine information and the understanding of biblical truths, unknown to the animal kingdom. By being "fearfully and wonderfully made," we are equipped to grasp the Spirit's messages as well as sense His compelling, awesome presence. That explains why we can hear His "still small voice" and decipher messages of peace or warning, conviction or guidance. God created us with that capacity.[1]

1. Charles R. Swindoll, *Flying Closer to the Flame* (Dallas, Tex.: Word Publishing, 1993), chap. 7.

How? Because we have been fearfully and wonderfully made in His image. We have been given a personality with a soul and a spirit that has the ability to think, feel, and choose. To penetrate beyond mere flesh and blood and reach the inner person, who we really are, the Spirit uses the Word of God, His sword, as it is described in Hebrews 4:12.

> For the word of God is living and active and sharper than any two-edged sword, and piercing as far as the division of soul and spirit, of both joints and marrow, and able to judge the thoughts and intentions of the heart.

"Amazing! As the Spirit ignites the fuel of God's written revelation, the flame bursts upon us and engulfs us with an inner awareness."[2]

Inner Promptings Then and Now

Let's turn now to "four biblical examples of the work of the Spirit . . . four occasions when the Spirit did a unique work in someone's life. And remember, if He did it then, He can do it today."[3]

1. *In times of loneliness and desperation, the Spirit prompts hope and encouragement.* Probably the one event people remember most about the Old Testament prophet Elijah is his victorious confrontation with the prophets of Baal on Mount Carmel (1 Kings 18). Coming down off that mountaintop, however, this lone prophet quickly descended into a wilderness of loneliness and despair. A death threat from Jezebel, the wicked wife of King Ahab, melted Elijah's bold faith into fear. And the man of God who had just gone toe to toe with four hundred pagan priests suddenly bolted like a frightened rabbit deep into the woods. Eventually he stopped beneath a juniper tree, not to pray for his faith to be strengthened, but for God to take his life before Jezebel did (19:1–4).

Rather than grant his distraught request, the Lord sent an angel to feed Elijah, who then put even more distance between himself and Jezebel by going to Horeb, the mountain of God. There the Lord ministered to His discouraged prophet.

2. Swindoll, *Flame*, chap. 7.
3. Swindoll, *Flame*, chap. 7.

He said, "Go forth, and stand on the mountain before the Lord." And behold, the Lord was passing by! And a great and strong wind was rending the mountains and breaking in pieces the rocks before the Lord; but the Lord was not in the wind. And after the wind an earthquake, but the Lord was not in the earthquake. And after the earthquake a fire, but the Lord was not in the fire; and after the fire a sound of gentle blowing. (vv. 11–12)

For centuries, "a sound of gentle blowing" has been rendered by the King James Bible as "a still small voice." Commentators Keil and Delitzsch explain it as a "gentle rustling. . . . It was in a soft, gentle rustling that He revealed Himself to him."[4]

Can you picture the scene? Elijah, wrapped in his desolation, loneliness, and despair, is standing there in the howling wind, looking at the fire, feeling the earthquake. But the Lord was in none of it. And all of a sudden those phenomena subside and there is this "delicate whispering voice." Somehow, deep within the prophet's heart he hears something from God. . . .

I am unable to explain how Elijah sensed God's voice or exactly what the Spirit said, but clearly He connected with the prophet.[5]

2. *In times of threatening fears, the Spirit prompts calm determination and courage.* The apostle Paul experienced such a time, recorded in Acts 20:22–23.

"And now, behold, bound in spirit, I am on my way to Jerusalem, not knowing what will happen to me there, except that the Holy Spirit solemnly testifies to me in every city, saying that bonds and afflictions await me."

4. C. F. Keil, "1 Kings," in *Commentary on the Old Testament in Ten Volumes*, by C. F. Keil and F. Delitzsch (reprint; Grand Rapids, Mich.: William B. Eerdmans Publishing Co., 1978), vol. 3, p. 258. The New International Version seems to strike a compromise by rendering it "a gentle whisper."

5. Swindoll, *Flame*, chap. 7.

These words were weighted with the wrenching emotions of one friend saying good-bye to another. The Apostle was leaving his close friends from the church at Ephesus with the realization that he would probably never see them again, because he was "bound in the Spirit" to go to Jerusalem.

> I think he means that he is "bound by the Holy Spirit" rather than being tied up in knots within his own spirit. In other words, he was captured in thoughts of, surrounded by the presence of, unable to get away from the reminders of God's heaven-sent Helper.[6]

And in this closeness, the Spirit continually revealed to Paul that trouble awaited him in that ancient Jewish city. But do you notice, there's not even a hint of fear in the Apostle's voice. How could this be? The next verse reveals his heart.

> "But I do not consider my life of any account as dear to myself, in order that I may finish my course, and the ministry which I received from the Lord Jesus, to testify solemnly of the gospel of the grace of God." (v. 24; see also Phil. 1:21)

"Strictly from the human viewpoint, when you and I know that trouble and afflictions await us, we are frightened. That does not occur when the Spirit of God brings a sense of reassurance."[7]

3. *In times of potential danger and disaster, the Spirit prompts inner reassurance.* A little later in Paul's life, the Apostle boarded a ship in Caesarea that was bound for Rome, where he would stand trial before Caesar. He was accompanied by Dr. Luke, whose log of the voyage in Acts 27 records one of the most exciting adventures in all the New Testament.

From the beginning, late summer winds hampered the trip, making progress slow and difficult. Several stops and days later, the ship finally put in at a place called Fair Havens on the island of Crete. The crew faced the decision of whether to winter in Fair Havens' unprotected harbor or risk pushing on to the safer port of Phoenix a little farther down the coast. The ship's pilot and captain voted for pushing on, but Paul warned against it: "Men, I perceive

6. Swindoll, *Flame*, chap. 7.
7. Swindoll, *Flame*, chap. 7.

that the voyage will certainly be attended with damage and great loss, not only of the cargo and the ship, but also of our lives" (v. 10). In the end, the Roman centurion in charge of the vessel was persuaded that they could make Phoenix (vv. 11–12). So they weighed anchor and set sail.

It wasn't long, however, before they were caught in the capricious hands of a violent wind. Scarcely able to steer the ship, they were constantly in danger of running aground on nearby shallows. The storm only grew more furious as the days passed, and soon they had to jettison the cargo and the ship's tackle just to stay afloat (vv. 13–19).

> And since neither sun nor stars appeared for many days, and no small storm was assailing us, from then on all hope of our being saved was gradually abandoned. (v. 20)

"The last and most precious cargo heaved overboard is the passengers' and crew's hope. They have exhausted every means for saving the ship, but to no avail. Now they simply huddle together, drifting in their own despair."[8] At that helpless moment, the apostle Paul addressed his shipmates with an uncanny confidence, saying,

> "Men, you ought to have followed my advice and not to have set sail from Crete, and incurred this damage and loss. And yet now I urge you to keep up your courage, for there shall be no loss of life among you, but only of the ship." (vv. 21b–22)

How could Paul, who was just as battered and tired as the rest of them, say something like this?

> It is the work of the Spirit of God that gives this kind of courage. It doesn't come naturally. . . .
> Paul verifies that his confidence came from the Lord. In fact, he says that he had been visited by an angel![9]

8. From the study guide *The Strength of an Exacting Passion: A Study of Acts 18:18–28:31*, coauthored by Bryce Klabunde, from the Bible-teaching ministry of Charles R. Swindoll (Anaheim, Calif.: Insight for Living, 1992), p. 138.

9. Swindoll, *Flame*, chap. 7.

Listen to the Apostle's words in verse 23–26:

> "For this very night an angel of the God to whom
> I belong and whom I serve stood before me, saying,
> 'Do not be afraid, Paul; you must stand before Cae-
> sar; and behold, God has granted you all those who
> are sailing with you.' Therefore, keep up your cour-
> age, men, for I believe God, that it will turn out
> exactly as I have been told."

Fifteen storm-tossed days later they did run aground on an island reef and the ship broke apart. Yet all 276 passengers managed to swim, paddle, and float to shore—soaked, but safe.

> How could Paul remain so encouraged? Because
> the Spirit of God, using an angelic messenger,
> prompted him to be confident in danger and to stand
> firm. . . . Such events may indeed be rare—per-
> haps only once or twice in a lifetime. But my point
> is this: Paul wasn't merely a brave man who loved
> challenges. He was prompted by God to be of good
> courage.[10]

4. *In times of great sorrow and pain, the Spirit ministers grace to us.* Let's join Paul in another setting now, where we'll see God's ministry amidst human misery.

> And because of the surpassing greatness of the reve-
> lations, for this reason, to keep me from exalting
> myself, there was given me a thorn in the flesh, a
> messenger of Satan to buffet me—to keep me from
> exalting myself! Concerning this I entreated the
> Lord three times that it might depart from me.
> (2 Cor. 12:7–8)

The Lord, however, though compassionate and caring toward His servant, told Paul "no" all three times. "But then God commu-nicated something to Paul's inner spirit that brought him an enor-mous sense of relief. I call this message another of the Spirit's 'inner promptings.' And what was it God made known to Paul in his pain? . . . Grace."[11]

10. Swindoll, *Flame*, chap. 7.
11. Swindoll, *Flame*, chap. 7.

And He has said to me, "My grace is sufficient for you, for power is perfected in weakness." (v. 9a)

"The God of all grace ministered grace to His hurting servant. Grace to endure. Grace to handle the pain. Grace to face the future. Grace to accept God's no. What a profound impact that had on the man!"[12]

> Most gladly, therefore, I will rather boast about my weaknesses, that the power of Christ may dwell in me. Therefore I am well content with weaknesses, with insults, with distresses, with persecutions, with difficulties, for Christ's sake; for when I am weak, then I am strong. (vv. 9b–10)

"When the Spirit of the Lord ministers grace, He prompts within us an unusual measure of divine strength. Somehow, in the mystery of His plan, He turns our pain into a platform upon which He does some of His best work."[13]

Two Practical Suggestions: Wise Guidelines worth Following

As we turn our attention from Elijah and Paul to the Spirit's work in our own lives, remember that *when you're not sure something is from the Spirit, tread softly.* Don't claim or presume the Spirit's leading in something that clearly contradicts the Scriptures. On the other hand, *when you are confident that it's of God, stand firm, even against other people's doubts.* "Be strong and resolute. That's a part of walking by faith. There are times when other people will say, "There is no way in the world that God could be in this," yet you know absolutely in your heart that He is. At times like that, simply stand firm. You won't be able to convince them, but that's all right. God is still doing unusual things. BUT don't get weird. You can be confident in God without becoming spooky or seeing lots of things no one else can see."[14]

---

12. Swindoll, *Flame*, chap. 7.
13. Swindoll, *Flame*, chap. 7.
14. Swindoll, *Flame*, chap. 7.

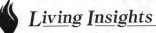

Has there ever been a time in your life when you felt an inner prompting from the Spirit? Describe it briefly.

_____

_____

_____

_____

Have you ever felt that the Spirit was prompting you to do something which later proved to be very foolish and immature? Don't bother to write this one out, because we've all had embarrassing experiences like that. You were absolutely sure, but as it turned out, you were also absolutely wrong. Maybe for you the consequences were simply that you felt a little foolish afterwards. For others, the results were nothing short of disastrous.

So how do we know when an "inner prompting" is from the Spirit? That's the rub. In non-moral issues and choices, the Scriptures don't provide detailed guidelines for discerning whether an impression comes from the Spirit or self or hormones or any number of other possible sources. So "a little caution is in order," writes Randall J. VanderMey in his book *God Talk:*

> If God speaks to me, as clearly as I'm speaking to you, his voice must have to carry above the din in that vast auditorium in my mind and body where hour after hour the sloppy rehearsals of daily life go on. I can make out some of the competing voices in there. . . . The scriptwriting team in my brain coaches me: "You should have said, 'OK, it's over.' That's what you should have said." . . . Guilt says, "What if they find out?" My "inner parents" say, "Check all the angles before you make a move." My inner child says, "That's mine and I want it." My inner tape says, "You don't deserve it." . . . Headlines, rules, catechism lessons, psychobabble, radio call-letters, molecules on my eardrums, the devil on one shoulder and the angel on the other, the music

of the spheres and the savage rumblings of monsters
of the deep. Voices, voices, voices.[15]

With so many voices auditioning for our attention, many Christians have decided that the safest thing to do is put their hands over their ears and shut everything out—including the Spirit. And the dispassionate stillness that ensues reinforces their belief that the Spirit dwelling inside them is silent.

But God is not silent, nor is His Spirit. Read the testimonies of past giants of the faith or ask any mature saint you know, and they all will tell you of those intimate moments in their lives when the Spirit's presence, leading, prompting, or whatever you want to call it, was unmistakably close and clear.

I know, I know—for those of us who like our faith neatly explained and securely controlled, this is an unpredictable, unverifiable, uncomfortable loose end. A thorn in our theology. But just remember dear friend, it just may be that this thorn, like Paul's, will serve a good purpose. Discerning the Spirit's presence and guidance in our lives isn't always easy. So where does that leave us? Continually seeking with all our hearts, souls, minds, and strength. That's exactly where He wants us to be, and that's exactly where we'll find Him.

15. Randall J. VanderMey, God Talk: The Triteness and Truth in Christian Clichés (Downers Grove, Ill.: InterVarsity Press, 1993), pp. 78–79.

Chapter 8

THE SPIRIT AND OUR EMOTIONS

Selected Scriptures

Have you noticed that the worship services in mainline Christian churches are often bland, dull, and emotionally flat?
How can it be that we who have the Spirit of the living God on
the inside appear so lifeless on the outside?

Am I suggesting we should all skip into church with smiles on
our faces as though life were one big happy lark? Of course not. I'm
just wondering—if life is really so difficult and God is really so
good, why do we respond to both with such an emotional detach-
ment? Where are the tears? Where is the joy? What's become of
our laughter and the expressions of our love? Who stole our passion?

Though we may be mature physically, many of us are stunted
emotionally. For too long we have kept this essential part of our
personality locked in a closet. And its absence has short-changed
our lives and our experience with the Holy Spirit.

How did it happen? Who's to blame? The culprit isn't a person.
Rather, it's a skewed perspective that puts down our feelings with
the dehumanizing dictum "Don't show your emotions." Over and
over again, since we were old enough to listen, we've been taught
to mistrust our emotions, to deny our emotions, to stuff them down
and be "brave little boys and girls." And, sadly, much of this same
message is repeated and reinforced among God's family members.
"Base your faith on facts, not feelings," we're told. And well we
should, for as Paul writes in Romans, "Faith comes from hearing,
and hearing by the word of Christ" (10:17). But does that mean
we're to have no emotions at all, that emotions are merely an
impediment to becoming Spirit-filled Christians?

No! On the contrary, without them we will never fully know
or glorify the Lord in all the deep, rich ways He has planned for
us. How could we? Intimacy can't flourish in an emotional vacuum.

As unpredictable and fluctuating as our emotions may be, we
must never forget that not only did God give us the capacity to
experience them, but, at times, He also works through the Spirit
to ignite them. And the result is often nothing short of electrifying.

God Has Made Us "Whole People"

Now some of you are already beginning to distance yourself from this study emotionally. You're pulling back and putting up defenses to keep us out and your feelings in. Perhaps you're afraid we'll ask you to go out and hug a stranger or do some other get-in-touch-with-your-feelings assignment. If so, *relax*. All we want you to do right now is turn to Genesis 1 for a very nonthreatening look at a theological foundation for feelings. *Then* we want you to go hug a stranger—just kidding! OK, on to Genesis 1.

As you read through the Creation account, you'll notice that the phrase "after their kind" is used repeatedly as God made the plants, trees, fish, birds, animals, and insects (vv. 11–12, 21, 24–25). But when it came to His crowning work, Adam and Eve, God patterned them after Himself. And all humanity since then bears the same unfading label—Made in His Image (vv. 26–27).

What does it mean to be made in God's image? The threads tying us together to resemble Him are not easily pulled apart and identified, but at least three are unmistakably visible.

First, *God has a mind and He created Adam and Eve with minds.* The first man and woman were endowed with intellects higher than all the other created life on earth. With this gift, Adam named the animals (2:20); he and Eve began a lifelong relationship of communicating with and understanding one another (v. 23); and, ultimately, this wonderful blessing was to enable both to know their Creator.

Second, *God has a heart and He created Adam and Eve with hearts.* By "heart" we don't mean the physical organ that pumps blood but the capacity to experience the full range of emotions. No doubt, Adam's heart pounded wildly when he first saw Eve. But more than that, he was overcome with the powerful emotion of love. On the other side of the spectrum are the feelings of fear and shame that suddenly panicked Adam and Eve when they sinned (chap. 3). Now, instead of drawing closer to the Lord, they both ran from Him and hid.

Third, *God has a will and He created Adam and Eve with wills.* Unlike the birds and the beasts that live by instinct, humankind has been blessed with volition—the ability to choose. We have the tremendous freedom and responsibility to make decisions. We can obey or not obey; it's completely up to us. For example, when God gave the command to eat from any tree of the garden except the tree of the knowledge of good and evil (2:16–17), it was still Adam and Eve's choice whether or not to obey that command. They chose not to obey, and ever since that same willful rebelliousness has been passed on to each of us.

Intertwined within the flesh and blood of our bodies are these three essential marks of God's image—mind, heart, and will. Without all three, we cannot function as the whole human beings our Father designed us to be. So if we suppress our emotions, we deliberately mar the beautiful image He has generously shared with us.

Surely, anyone who has seen the Spirit of God bring conviction, relief, or joy in a revival can appreciate the value of emotions. The great Puritan preacher Jonathan Edwards certainly did. He ministered throughout New England during the Great Awakening in the 1700s and came to this conclusion:

> I am bold to assert that no change of religious nature will ever take place unless the affections are moved. Without this, no natural man will earnestly seek for his salvation. Without this, there is no wrestling with God in prayer for mercy. No one is humbled and brought to the feet of God unless he has seen for himself his own unworthiness. No one will ever be induced to fly in refuge to Christ as long as his heart remains unaffected. Likewise, no saint has been weaned out of the cold and lifeless state of mind, or recovered from backsliding, without having his heart affected. In summary, nothing significant ever changed the life of anyone when the heart was not deeply affected.[1]

The Significant Presence of Our Feelings

In making us like Himself, God gave us a kaleidoscope of emotions. Perhaps for those of you who are still reluctant to acknowledge their presence, a brief glimpse from the Scriptures will open your eyes to the varying hues of His handiwork.

1. Jonathan Edwards, *Religious Affections*, abridged ed., Classics of Faith and Devotion series (Portland, Oreg.: Multnomah Press, 1984), pp. 10–11.

A List of God-Given Emotions

The range of emotions in the Scriptures that God affirms, affects, touches, moves through, changes, and ignites is amazing. For example:

cheerfulness (2 Cor. 9:7)
love (2 Tim. 1:7; 1 John 4:19)
hatred, devotion, fervency, joy, sadness, haughtiness,
    and peace (Rom. 12:9–18)
fear/respect (Prov. 1:7)
gratitude (Pss. 146–150)
annoyance (Acts 16:18)
grief (Eph. 4:30)
tenderheartedness (Eph. 4:32)
perplexity (2 Cor. 4:8)
anger (Eph. 4:26; Matt. 23:13–33)
anxiety (Matt. 6:31–34)

These are but a smattering of the feelings that are constantly shifting in ever-changing patterns within each of us. Christ Himself wept with grief, was moved with compassion, rejoiced, trembled with anger, felt troubled, and prayed with an intensity that left sweat pouring from Him as if it were blood flowing from a wound. That's passion, my friend. Jesus had it, He expressed it, and He wants you and me to do the same. We must open the closed doors of our austere intellectualism and allow our emotions to take their rightful place in our lives. Let yourself love. Be tenderhearted. Feel grief and sadness. Be the vibrant image bearer God meant you to be, not a sterile witness to some dusty theology.

Some Necessary Warnings We Need to Heed

As in every endeavor, flying closer to the flame emotionally has its own peculiar hazards. So let us guide you past three in particular so that you don't get burned.

1. *Intellectualism:* This is a spiritless pattern of living some people veer into when they rely strictly on their intellect and refuse to allow emotion to serve its proper function.

2. *Emotionalism:* Many sincere Christians have gone to the opposite extreme of making emotions the guiding compass of their lives. They fly by the seat of their emotional experiences instead of clear biblical doctrines.

3. *Fanaticism*: A third flight path destined for trouble is excessive and intense devotion that lacks balance, discernment, and wisdom. If you notice these signs—an exclusionary spirit, paranoid reactions, absolute obedience to a single authority figure, absence of openness to criticism, or truth taken to an extreme—then know you need to change directions *immediately*! You're on a crash course with a cult.

Some "Traditional Sayings" We Need to Clarify

As Christians, many of us have never been able to fly closer to the flame emotionally because we could never get this part of our personality off the ground. Too many traditional sayings are blocking the runway for us to take off. So let's close our time together by clearing away some of these obstacles.

"Never trust your feelings." Remember that one? It's the word *never* that causes many of us to stumble every time we strain to fly. But consider this: if peace is one of the affirmations God gives us when we follow His will, is it right to say that we should never trust that emotion? Or how about when the Spirit convicts us of wrong and we feel guilty. Should we not trust and appreciate that?

"Experience proves nothing." Many of us have not only heard this one, we've also passed it along. And while it is true that there is a danger of reinterpreting the Scriptures on the basis of our experiences, it is not true that experience has nothing to teach us. Many of life's most invaluable lessons are learned in the crucible of experience.

"Experience is your best teacher." When applied to our emotions, this oft-repeated maxim leads many into the error of emotionalism: following our feelings instead of Scripture. To avoid that trap, we need to remember that *guided* experience is our best teacher. Let the Word of God be our rule for interpreting life's experiences. And in those times when no moral decision is at stake, when we're facing a crucial career choice, for example, remember these wise words from Proverbs:

> Without consultation, plans are frustrated,
> But with many counselors they succeed. (15:22)

"Let your conscience be your guide." The reliability of our conscience depends a great deal on its condition. If this inner moral compass has been dulled or hardened because of sin or has been overly sensitized because of abusive shaming, our intimacy with the Spirit will be thrown off course.

With these obstacles out of the way, you're now clear for takeoff. We want to thank you for choosing us to help you on your journey toward the Spirit and your emotions. Please fasten your seat belts and have an adventuresome, exciting, unforgettable flight—closer to the flame.

 ## Living Insights

Where would we be if God's great love had not moved Him to sacrifice His Son for our salvation? Where would we be if Jesus hadn't compassionately humbled Himself to the excruciating point of a Roman crucifixion? What would have happened to the early church if Paul had not been motivated by the love of Christ to preach the gospel to the Gentiles? Where would the church be today if Luther had not been angered enough to nail his ninety-five theses to the door of the Castle Church in 1517?

How horrific would the Holocaust have been if Churchill hadn't inspired millions of others to hold on with his same bulldog determination? What would be the plight of the poor in India today without the tender mercy poured out through Mother Teresa?

Indeed, what great achievement has ever been accomplished without the motivating presence of emotion? Could you imagine a Savior without love or a Paul without passion? How about an apathetic Martin Luther King Jr.?

What great deed of kindness or courage will be left undone in your life if you divorce the truth of God's Word from the emotions it inspires?

 ## Living Insights

Dear Brother or Sister in Christ:

Emotion is not your enemy—apathy is. For it's when we see suffering or injustice and it no longer moves us that we are in the most danger of becoming the least human. It's when evil triumphs over good and we simply stare with cold, dispassionate eyes that the world understandably reasons, "There must be no right or wrong, no truth, no God."

Apathy is a sickness that leads to emotional death. Your feelings become blunted, leaving behind a living corpse with no emotional pulse. Has this happened to you? Are you trying so hard to control and suppress certain feelings that you're smothering an essential part of your personality?

Many of us are doing so because we grew up in homes that condemned certain emotions as unacceptable. Anger, for example, of any kind, is often one of the biggies that's taboo around Christians. Looking back, were certain emotions considered off-limits in your family?

_____

_____

_____

_____

_____

_____

Are you still struggling to accept and express any of the emotions you've listed?

_____

_____

_____

_____

_____

What strange people we become when we successfully suffocate the precious gift God has given us. Surely this deadened state is not what He would call Spirit-filled living. If you, like a great many of us, need help in resurrecting your emotions, we recommend the following:

Cloud, Henry. *Changes That Heal: How to Understand Your Past to Ensure a Healthier Future*. Grand Rapids, Mich.: Zondervan Publishing House, 1990.

Seamands, David A. *Healing for Damaged Emotions*. Wheaton, Ill.: Scripture Press Publications, Victor Books, 1981.

Chapter 9

THINKING THEOLOGICALLY ABOUT SICKNESS AND HEALING

Selected Scriptures

Splash! Joni Eareckson dove into the Chesapeake Bay a strong, athletic young girl. Seconds later, she was paralyzed from the neck down, completely helpless, and still under water. Though rescued from drowning by her sister, the doctors could not rescue Joni from the paralysis that swept over her body.

Joni came to accept the fact that she couldn't be healed—medically. But what about God? Didn't Christ heal all kinds of paralysis and sickness? The more Joni thought and prayed about these things, the more she became convinced God would heal her too. So,

> she brought together a group of friends and church leaders and set up a private healing service. The week before that service, she publicly confessed her faith by telling people, "Watch for me standing on your doorstep soon; I'm going to be healed." On the scheduled day the group read Scriptures, anointed her with oil and prayed in fervent faith. Today, fifteen years later, she is still a quadriplegic. . . . [She] did everything right and seemed to have met all the conditions, yet she was not healed.[1]

Was Joni denied this miracle because she didn't have enough faith? Some believe so. Others say she wasn't healed because of unconfessed sin in her life. Still others would quibble over the healing technique she used, promoting instead their own three-step process.

This chapter has been adapted from "Suffering, Sickness, Sin—and Healing," in the study guide *James: Practical and Authentic Living,* coauthored by Lee Hough, from the Bible-teaching ministry of Charles R. Swindoll (Fullerton, Calif.: Insight for Living, 1991).

1. Bruce Barron, *The Health and Wealth Gospel* (Downers Grove, Ill.: InterVarsity Press, 1987), p. 126.

What do *you* think?

Thousands travel around the world seeking those who claim to have the gift of healing. Testimonies of people declaring they have been healed by the Spirit abound. Special "anointed" cloths have even been sold that were said to have healing powers. Are these things real? What about the use of medicine? Should we trust God alone for healing? Does God heal? If so, is there a particular method we should follow? What about those who aren't healed? What about Joni?

The issue of the Spirit and divine healing today is a highly charged, hotly debated one that more often than not leaves people feeling lost in a forest of unanswered questions. If you're having trouble finding your way, come with us as we seek some clear direction from the compass of God's Word.

Possible Sources of "Phenomenal Events"

For the sake of clarification, let's begin by identifying a few key sources that might produce a supernatural or an alleged supernatural manifestation.[2]

First: *The manifestation could be self-induced.* In today's stressful world, a great many people have psychosomatic illnesses, physical sickness brought about by mental or emotional disturbances. Resolve that underlying cause, and what often passes as a "miraculous healing" is actually a natural psychological one. The change is real and it's wonderful, but it is not the direct result of divine, supernatural intervention.

Second: *The phenomenon could find its source in highly charged emotional meetings.* Every generation has its sad examples of preachers who rely less on the Holy Spirit and more on manipulative hype to produce spectacular miracles of healing. Mass hysteria and hypnosis, the power of suggestion, brainwashing—these techniques work, and there are plenty of pious pretenders using them right now to fleece the gullible.

Third: *The source could be satanic.* Never naively assume that something is heaven-sent simply because it appears to be miraculous. Just because someone claims to be a minister of the gospel does not guarantee that his or her message and power are of the

---

2. Adapted from John White's *When the Spirit Comes with Power* (Downers Grove, Ill.: InterVarsity Press, 1988), pp. 60–61.

Lord. That is not always so. As in the apostle Paul's day, the church today is infiltrated with

> false apostles, deceitful workers, disguising themselves as apostles of Christ. And no wonder, for even Satan disguises himself as an angel of light. (2 Cor. 11:13–14)

Satan has power too. And if he can use it to enable charlatans who will deceive the saved as well as the unsaved, you can bet he will.

Fourth: *The source could, in fact, be God.* Surely, no Christian who has read God's Word would question His power to heal or that He has done so. The testimony of the Scriptures and reliable church history gives indisputable evidence to both.

Instead of launching into any of those thrilling stories, however, let's do what many who seek answers about healings fail to do, and that is gain a clear understanding of the relationship between sin and sickness, spiritual health and physical health.

Foundational Facts regarding Sin and Sickness

When God created Adam and Eve, the first couple enjoyed a world completely free from sin and its corrupting influence. But from the moment they disobeyed God in the Garden, the battle with selfishness, suffering, and death began. What are the ramifications for you and me? Here are six important facts to remember.

1. *Primarily, there are two types of sin—original and personal.* Original sin refers to the sin nature we inherited from Adam (Rom. 5:12–21). Personal sin is the daily disobedience that is spawned by our Adamic nature (7:14–23). Original sin is the root; personal sin is the fruit.

2. *Original sin introduced sickness, suffering, and death to the human race.* The consequences attached to our inheritance of Adam's sinful nature are summed up in Romans 5:

> Therefore, just as through one man sin entered into the world, and death through sin, and so death spread to all men, because all sinned. (v. 12; see also 6:23; 1 Cor. 15:21a; Ezek. 18:4b)

3. *Often, there exists a direct relationship between personal sins and physical sickness.* Remember the story of David and Bathsheba in 2 Samuel 11 and 12? David committed adultery with Bathsheba, arranged her husband's death, then refused to acknowledge his sin

for some time. Finally, after a rebuke from the prophet Nathan, David confessed and repented. Psalm 32 journals the physical sufferings he endured during the time of his rebellion.

> When I kept silent about my sin, my body wasted
> away
> Through my groaning all day long.
> For day and night Thy hand was heavy upon me;
> My vitality was drained away as with the fever heat
> of summer. (vv. 3–4)[3]

4. *Sometimes there is no relationship between personal sins and human afflictions.* Once, when the disciples and Jesus passed by a blind man, they asked Him,

> "Rabbi, who sinned, this man or his parents, that he should be born blind?" Jesus answered, "It was neither that this man sinned, nor his parents; but it was in order that the works of God might be displayed in him." (John 9:2b–3)

5. *Sometimes it is not God's will that we be healed.* Paul had the gift of healing (Acts 20:7–12; 28:7–9), yet he left Trophimus sick in Miletus (2 Tim. 4:20); Epaphroditus almost died while ministering to the Apostle (Phil. 2:25–27); Paul's spiritual son Timothy had a stomach problem and "frequent ailments" (1 Tim. 5:23); and Paul himself was told by God that his "thorn in the flesh" would remain (2 Cor. 12:7–9a).

Typically, those who claim that it's God's will for everyone to be healed base their belief on the last phrase of Isaiah 53:5, "And by His scourging we are healed." However, the context of this verse refers to spiritual health, not physical. Peter underscored this when he wrote,

> He Himself bore our sins in His body on the cross,
> that we might die to sin and live to righteousness;
> for by His wounds you were healed. (1 Pet. 2:24)

6. *On other occasions, it is God's will that we be healed, and He does so.*

Let's pause here to let the broad theological foundation we've just poured have time to set in our minds. Once you're ready, we'll

3. Another example of this principle is found in 1 Corinthians 11:23–30.

build on this basic understanding of sin and sickness in chapter 10 by examining the apostle James' recommended procedure for "restoring the one who is sick" (James 5:15).

 ## Living Insights

> And when I came to you, brethren, I did not come with superiority of speech or of wisdom, proclaiming to you the testimony of God. For I determined to know nothing among you except Jesus Christ, and Him crucified. And I was with you in weakness and in fear and in much trembling. And my message and my preaching were not in persuasive words of wisdom, but in demonstration of the Spirit and of power, that your faith should not rest on the wisdom of men, but on the power of God. (1 Cor. 2:1–5)

This was, perhaps, the world's greatest evangelist—the apostle Paul. Take a good look at him. What do you see? Did he come to Corinth (or anywhere else for that matter) with a lot of hype? Did he have a slick image and a packaged presentation? Were his words rehearsed, as well as his emotions? Is there anything revealed here about this man or his ministry that would lead you to believe he brainwashed people into believing his message or the miracles he performed?

John White, in his book *When the Spirit Comes with Power*, describes how brainwashing can occur:

> If you want to manipulate people, work on their input levels. Scream the gospel at them for a while. Then to keep them off balance switch to a quiet, intimate joke or two. Then start shrieking again. Your audience will soon get a high anxiety level and be putty in your hands.[4]

A little later, White adds:

> To manipulate a large number of people you need

---

4. White, *When the Spirit Comes with Power*, p. 67.

to exhaust them, to bombard them with levels of sensation they are not accustomed to, to expose them to concepts that frighten them, to humiliate them and make them feel guilty and hopeless, while still offering a new and magical idea. Crowd effect will be on your side, in that the crowd tends to carry individuals along with it.[5]

Could brainwashing explain the conversions, the miraculous healings, or the general influence of Paul's ministry? Of course not. Could it explain, however, what's happening in the ministry of many so-called healers who peddle the Holy Spirit today? Could it explain what's happening in the meetings and seminars of someone you're following now?

Think about it. Think about it hard, "lest as the serpent deceived Eve by his craftiness, your minds should be led astray from the simplicity and purity of devotion to Christ" (2 Cor. 11:3).

 Living Insights   STUDY TWO

Today when people talk of being healed by the Spirit, the conversation always seems to focus exclusively on the physical. But in doing so, we are ignoring another crucial aspect of the Spirit's healing ministry—conviction of sin (see John 16:8).

Sin is like a poisonous infection. When we allow it to fester unconfessed, it spreads throughout our bodies, our minds, our emotions, even our relationships with others. Through the cleansing work of the Spirit, we're reminded of the wrongs we've committed and are prompted to seek forgiveness—healing.

Is there a particular sin that needs confessing in order to bring healing to your tortured conscience? Is your vitality drained away because of sexual immorality? Is your body wasting away because of bitterness and hate? Do you groan under the awful weight of the consequences of your hidden sin? King Solomon understood the sickness of soul and body that you feel, and he wrote,

> Do not be wise in your own eyes;
> Fear the Lord and turn away from evil.

5. White, *When the Spirit Comes with Power*, pp. 67–68.

It will be healing to your body,
And refreshment to your bones. (Prov. 3:7–8)

If the Spirit is convicting you of a particular sin, then let these words poured out from David's heart in Psalm 41:4 lead you into a time of confession and healing.

"O Lord, be gracious to me;
Heal my soul, for I have sinned against Thee . . ."

Chapter 10

A BIBLICAL CASE FOR HEALING

James 5:13–16

"I s anyone among you suffering?" wrote one of the apostles, "Let him pray. . . . Is anyone among you sick? Let him . . ."

Let him what? What would you recommend? Some homemade elixir? Plenty of rest and vitamin C? Perhaps a poultice, a favorite faith healer, or the telephone number of a medical specialist?

To find out what remedy the Holy Spirit inspired James to write, let's turn to the fifth chapter of his epistle.

Following the Steps Prescribed in Scripture

Clearly, as we read James' instructions in verses 13–15, he has two patients in mind, two categories of people in pain. If you'll just step into his office with us now, we'll listen in on the specific treatment he prescribes for each.

Those Who Are "Suffering"

> Is anyone among you suffering? Let him pray.
> (James 5:13a)

The Greek term for *suffering* here literally means "in distress." It's a broad term that can mean anxiety or some affliction from which there is no immediate relief. James tells this person, "Pray!" He doesn't promise an answer of healing, though it may come. But if it doesn't, God's grace and strength is infused in the petitioner who prays diligently so that he or she might be able to say with Paul,

> most gladly, therefore, I will rather boast about my weaknesses, that the power of Christ may dwell in me. Therefore I am well content with weaknesses, with insults, with distresses, with persecutions, with

---

This chapter has been adapted from "Suffering, Sickness, Sin—and Healing," in the study guide *James: Practical and Authentic Living*, coauthored by Lee Hough, from the Bible-teaching ministry of Charles R. Swindoll (Fullerton, Calif.: Insight for Living, 1991).

difficulties, for Christ's sake; for when I am weak, then I am strong. (2 Cor. 12:9b–10)

Those Who Are "Sick"

Moving ahead to verse 14 of chapter 5, James introduces the problem of physical illness.

> Is anyone among you sick? Let him call for the elders of the church, and let them pray over him, anointing him with oil in the name of the Lord. (v. 14)[1]

The Greek term for *sick* used here means "without strength." It is the idea of being totally incapacitated. What does James recommend in this situation?

First, the one who is sick should take the initiative and summon the elders of the church. There's no way anyone can know you're sick unless you tell them. And yet many expect everyone to somehow know, and then they complain when nobody comes to help. When we become seriously ill, our first step is to make others aware of our need.

Second, the elders are to carry out two functions: anoint and pray (v. 14). The Greek construction of this sentence actually states, "Let them pray over him, *having anointed* him with oil in the name of the Lord." The anointing should precede the praying.

Typically, the word *anoint* is associated with a religious ceremony where oil is applied to the head, as we saw in chapter 6 of our study. But, as Jay Adams points out in his book *Competent to Counsel,*

> James did not write about ceremonial anointing at all. . . . The ordinary word for a ceremonial anointing was *chrio* (a cognate of *christos* [Christ] the "anointed One"). The word James used (*aleipho*), in contrast to the word *chrio* ("to anoint"), usually means "to rub" or simply "apply." The word *aleipho* was used to describe the personal application of salves, lotions, and perfumes, which usually had an oil base. . . . [Related to this word is] an *aleiptes*

---

1. Some people believe verse 14 teaches that the clergy are to go to the dying and administer last rites using oil and a special liturgy. However, this passage concerns healing and not dying; restoring to health, not passing away. Others take the view that this verse applied only to the apostles of the first-century church. But James addressed elders, not apostles or "healers"; therefore, it still applies.

[who] was a "trainer" who rubbed down athletes in a gymnastic school. *Aleipho* was used frequently in medical treatises. And so it turns out that what James required by the use of oil was the use of the best medical means of the day. James simply said to rub oil . . . on the body, and pray. . . . In this passage he urged the treating of sickness by medical means accompanied by prayer. The two are to be used together; neither to the exclusion of the other. So instead of teaching faith healing apart from the use of medicine, the passage teaches just the opposite.[2]

Fortunately, our medical expertise has improved from oil to antibiotics, X rays, and laser surgery. And just as the elders in James' day were to see that proper medical treatment was applied, so elders today are to do the same.

Third, James recommends that the sick leave the results in God's hands. The elders were to anoint and pray over the sick "in the name of the Lord" (v. 14b), invoking God's will for the situation. And

when it is His sovereign will to bring healing, it will occur. And in that case, "the prayer offered in faith will restore the one."

The Greek word here translated "restore" is *sōzō*. It means "to save." So the prayer offered in faith will literally save the sick person's life. Why? Because in that case it is God's will for healing to occur. . . .

There is another important term here: "The Lord *will raise* him up." This looks miraculous to me . . . a case of instantaneous healing. And don't overlook the additional comment: "if he has committed sins, they will be forgiven him."

Perhaps the person's past was marked by sins— extended, serious sins. If this was the root of the problem, there will be an admission of it in the process of the healing.[3]

2. Jay E. Adams, *Competent to Counsel* (Phillipsburg, N.J.: Presbyterian and Reformed Publishing Co., 1970), pp. 107–8. Compare Mark 16:1 and John 12:3–7 regarding ceremonial anointing with Luke 10:33b–34a, which refers to medical anointing.

3. Charles R. Swindoll, *Flying Closer to the Flame* (Dallas, Tex.: Word Publishing, 1993), chap. 10

Several Practical Principles to Claim

In summary, we can glean four practical measures to follow—two from verse 16 and two from our passage as a whole.

> Therefore, confess your sins to one another, and pray for one another, so that you may be healed. The effective prayer of a righteous man can accomplish much. (v. 16)

First: *Confession of sin is healthy—employ it.* Don't let sins build up in your life to the point that they make you physically ill. William Barclay writes,

> In a very real sense it is easier to confess sins to God than to confess them to men; and yet in sin there are two barriers to be removed—the barrier it sets up between us and God, and the barrier it sets up between us and our fellow-men. If both these barriers are to be removed, both kinds of confession must be made.[4]

Second: *Praying for one another is essential—practice it.* An appropriate response to your friends' confessions would be to lift them up to the Lord in prayer. Let these companions know that you are willing to enter into their struggle; let them hear your love and support being poured out on their behalf before the throne of God.

Third: *Use of medical assistance is imperative—obey it.* Asking others to pray for your physical healing while ignoring proper medical treatment is not spiritual; it's foolish. Someone may rightly ask, "Why should I pray for your healing if you're not willing to do all that God commands, like seeking medical assistance?"

Fourth: *When healing comes from God—claim it.* Whether or not an illness is the result of personal sin, when God heals, remember to thank Him and give Him the glory!

A Final Word

Did you notice that James never once mentions "faith healers"? When we're sick, James urges us to call for the leaders in our local assembly. And it makes no difference what their spiritual gifts are.

---

4. William Barclay, *The Letters of James and Peter,* rev. ed., The Daily Study Bible Series (Philadelphia, Pa.: Westminster Press, 1976), p. 131.

In conclusion, here are Chuck's own convictions on this important topic.

> I believe in divine healing. I do not believe in divine healers. I believe in faith healing. I do not believe in faith healers. There is a great difference. I believe that God in His sovereign grace and power will in fact reach down in some cases and change a condition. . . . And I am of the conviction that God does that apart from any individual who claims to have certain powers.[5]

 ## Living Insights

If you are struggling with sickness even after following James' prescription, perhaps you need to look at his counsel in verse 16— confession of sin. Could personal sin be the cause of some of your physical problems? Have repressed anger or guilt caused you some sleepless nights, headaches, ulcers, or anxiety attacks?

To help diagnose your condition, set aside some time to pray through David's words in Psalm 139, and search your own heart and thoughts for any "hurtful way" that needs to be confessed.

> Search me, O God, and know my heart;
> Try me and know my anxious thoughts;
> And see if there be any hurtful way in me,
> And lead me in the everlasting way. (vv. 23–24)[6]

Diagnostic Confession

_____

_____

_____

_____

5. Charles R. Swindoll, "Suffering, Sickness, Sin—and Healing." Sermon given at the First Evangelical Free Church of Fullerton, California, January 5, 1975.

6. For those of you who are in the merciless hands of an unrelenting illness, please know that we are not assuming that personal sin is the root of all suffering. As we saw clearly in John 9:1–3, there is sometimes no relationship between sin and sickness.

_____

_____

_____ _____

_____

_____

 Living Insights

Nowadays many of us are so confused about the topic of healing that we have a tendency to go to extremes. For example, some of us back away from seeking medical help and rely instead on the premise that if we pray in faith expecting God to heal, He will. Then, too, there are those of us who run to the doctor without ever giving prayer for healing a second thought. It's too religious, too farfetched to believe that God would actually heal.

In his essay "Faith-Healing and the Sovereignty of God," C. Everett Koop challenges us with this insightful perspective:

> A surprising number of Christians are convinced God will not be believed unless He makes tumors disappear, causes asthma to go away, and pops eyes into empty sockets. But the gospel is accepted by God-given faith, not by the guarantee that you will never be sick, or, if you are, that you will be miraculously healed. God is the Lord of healing, of growing, of weather, of transportation, and of every other process. Yet people don't expect vegetables without plowing. They don't expect levitation instead of getting in a car and turning a key—even for extraordinarily good and exceptional reasons.
>
> Although God *could* do all of this, Christian airline pilots do not fly straight into a thunderstorm after asking God for a safe corridor, although He could give them such safety. We do not have public services and ask God to remove all criminals, prostitutes, and pornographers from our midst, although He could do that too. God *could* eliminate AIDS

from our planet. While we pray for a speedy discovery of successful treatment, I must do all I can to employ medical science in its task.[7]

Are you struggling with sickness right now? Then don't be afraid to approach the Lord of healing through prayer. Neither be afraid to seek help from the medical profession. It just may be that if He doesn't heal you miraculously, He may decide to heal you through the use of medicine. Don't limit Him as to how or when He might want to heal you.

7. C. Everett Koop, "Faith-Healing and the Sovereignty of God," in *The Agony of Deceit*, ed. Michael Horton (Chicago, Ill.: Moody Press, 1990), pp. 173–74.

Chapter 11

WHEN THE SPIRIT BRINGS A SLOW RECOVERY

Acts 28:1—10

"Healing is a matter of time,"[1] wrote the renowed Greek physician Hippocrates. And the deeper the wound, physically or emotionally, the greater the amount of time we need to heal. In light of our "instant everything" world,

> that may not sound very encouraging . . . but it is, more often than not, true. . . .
> . . . [Throughout my years in] ministry I have had a great deal of contact with people who hurt.
> . . .
> . . . Other ministers, it seems, enjoy the role of leading people into rather rapid relief of their pain. Admittedly, I could easily envy such a joyful and popular ministry. More often than not, it seems my lot to help those who do not "heal in a hurry," no matter how hard they try, no matter how firmly they believe, no matter how sincerely they pray.[2]

Though it isn't nearly as exciting as a miraculous healing, there are times when the Spirit brings a slow recovery. Such a time of convalescence came at a crucial hour in the apostle Paul's life. On his way to face trial in Rome, the Apostle's ship was caught in a violent storm. For days, everyone on board went without food or rest in what seemed like a hopeless situation. Finally, the battered ship struck a reef, spilling its cargo of exhausted passengers into the

This chapter has been adapted from "Time to Heal," in the study guide The Strength of an Exacting Passion: A Study of Acts 18:18–28:31, coauthored by Bryce Klabunde, from the Bible-teaching ministry of Charles R. Swindoll (Anaheim, Calif.: Insight for Living, 1992).

1. Hippocrates, Precepts, as quoted in Bartlett's Familiar Quotations, 15th ed., rev. and enl., ed. Emily Morison Beck (Boston, Mass.: Little, Brown and Co., 1980), p. 79.

2. Charles R. Swindoll, Recovery: When Healing Takes Time (Waco, Tex.: Word Books, Publisher, 1985), pp. 8, 10, 11.

frothing surf of a Mediterranean island. Though they littered the beach like so much human debris, all 276 people made it to shore alive. The storm, however, had taken a tremendous physical and emotional toll on everyone. They were going to need time to heal—and lots of it.

Let's join Dr. Luke in Acts 28 as he describes that unique period of recovery.

Initial Orientation

With waterlogged sluggishness, the beached survivors slowly regrouped themselves to ask the obvious—where were they? The answer was Malta (v. 1), a rugged island some eighteen miles long and eight miles wide located about fifty miles south of Sicily. In that day, the island's name was actually Melita, which was "the Canaanite word for 'refuge.'"[3] Can you believe that? Paul and company had literally run aground on an island of shelter and seclusion—God's private room reserved for His servants' recuperation. But the Apostle didn't while away his entire time there sipping coconut juice under a palm tree. As we shall see, he used his healing time as an opportunity to help others find healing as well.

Personal Treatment

The stranded travelers immediately made contact with the islanders, whom Luke calls "natives"—barbaros in Greek (v. 2a), from which we get our word barbarian.[4] Far from being crude or hostile, however, the local inhabitants were compassionate toward their unexpected guests.

Extraordinary Kindness

The natives showed us extraordinary kindness; for because of the rain that had set in and because of the cold, they kindled a fire and received us all. (v. 2)

3. F. F. Bruce, Commentary on the Book of the Acts, The New International Commentary on the New Testament series (Grand Rapids, Mich.: William B. Eerdmans Publishing Co., 1954), p. 521.

4. "To the Greek the barbarian was a man who said bar-bar, that is, a man who spoke an unintelligible foreign language and not the beautiful Greek tongue." William Barclay, The Acts of the Apostles, rev. ed., The Daily Study Bible Series (Philadelphia, Pa.: Westminster Press, 1976), p. 187.

How warm—emotionally as well as physically—that fire must have felt to those sodden seafarers. Its comforting crackle and the friendly faces of the islanders ignited a flicker of hope and happiness where there had only been despair. God's healing process had begun.

Unjust Criticism

The peaceful scene changes, however, with the lightning strike of calamity.

> When Paul had gathered a bundle of sticks and laid them on the fire, a viper came out because of the heat, and fastened on his hand. And when the natives saw the creature hanging from his hand, they began saying to one another, "Undoubtedly this man is a murderer, and though he has been saved from the sea, justice has not allowed him to live." (vv. 3–4)

A chill suddenly douses the warmth of their reception as the superstitious islanders construe Paul's snakebite to be a sign of punishment. Guilty by reason of catastrophe—does that reasoning ring any bells? Isn't that exactly the same kind of logic Job's friends applied to his suffering? "Your wickedness is great," they said, "that's why God is punishing you with adversity" (see Job 22).

Interestingly enough, this mind-set is not limited to just Job's friends or a few first-century islanders. Many Christians today endure not only the hardship of a sea of troubles but also the pain of venomous attacks from others who accuse them of sin. Calamity is proof of guilt, critics claim, as they wag their viperous tongues.

Please, please, don't jump to conclusions about those who are suffering and add to their woes by presuming their guilt. Snakebites don't prove wrongdoing any more than hard times always imply hidden sin.

Unfortunately, it was too late for the islanders. Their minds were made up. Paul was guilty and the sentence of death had been delivered—or so they thought.

Inappropriate Exaltation

> They were expecting that he was about to swell up or suddenly fall down dead. But after they had waited a long time and had seen nothing unusual happen to him, they changed their minds and began to say that he was a god. (Acts 28:6)

The natives were amazed. Paul's unaffected health confounded their superstitious system of justice. "Maybe he's not a murderer after all," they whispered to each other. But what then? "Maybe," someone gasped, "maybe he's not a man!"

From a murderer to a god—the people's opinion of Paul leaped from one extreme to the other. As for the Apostle, Luke doesn't record that he responded with a single word. It seems he humbly ignored all the hubbub and quietly went about the business of resting and healing—which, interestingly, opened up some opportunities for God to use him in the healing of others.

Relational Concern

The first opportunity arose when a prominent Roman invited Paul and his companions for a visit.

Instant Healing

> Now in the neighborhood of that place were lands belonging to the leading man of the island, named Publius, who welcomed us and entertained us courteously three days. And it came about that the father of Publius was lying in bed afflicted with recurrent fever and dysentery; and Paul went in to see him and after he had prayed, he laid his hands on him and healed him. (vv. 7–8)

News of this miraculous healing spread quickly over the island, and it wasn't long before the Apostle had a waiting room full of patients.

Prolonged Recovery

> And after this had happened, the rest of the people on the island who had diseases were coming to him and getting cured. (v. 9)

In his commentary on Acts, William Barclay writes,

> In verse 9 there is a very interesting possibility. That verse says that the rest of the people who had ailments came and *were healed*. The word used is the word for *receiving medical attention*; and there are scholars who think that this can well mean, not only that they came to Paul, but that they came to Luke

who gave them of his medical skill. If that be so, this passage gives us the earliest picture we possess of the work of a *medical missionary*.[5]

Practical Lessons

From the time they first washed ashore to when they finally sailed away, three peaceful months of healing took place on the island of refuge. Three months of quiet refreshment and restoration. Three months of ministering to those islanders whose bodies had suffered shipwreck because of some disease. What a wonderful respite for everyone. And when it was time for Paul and his companions to depart, Luke remembers how the natives, some of whom they had probably saved from death,

> honored us with many marks of respect; and when we were setting sail, they supplied us with all we needed. (v. 10)

As you imagine the Mediterranean trade winds billowing the sails that will carry Paul from his island of refuge to Rome, remember these two lessons for your own times of healing.

First, *the one who takes time to heal should be respected, not resented.* Although falsely accused at first, the people quickly learned to respect Paul during his stay on the island. Concerning those we know who are recovering from emotional shipwrecks, we, too, must respect their needs and be patient with them during their sometimes tortuous road back to health.

Second, *the one who is healed will be better equipped to help others.* Enduring emotional storms and experiencing God's healing afterward make us real to others. We can say honestly to people recovering from similar ordeals, "I know how you feel; God helped me through, and He can help you too."

 Living Insights   STUDY ONE

Former major league pitcher Dave Dravecky was thrown an unexpected curve called cancer that resulted in the amputation of

---

5. Barclay, *The Acts of the Apostles*, p. 189.

his pitching arm. If that weren't enough suffering, he then had to face the curve of condemnation.

> I was in Grand Rapids, Michigan, speaking at a chapel service when I was approached by a man in his twenties. He told me I had cancer because there was sin in my life. He told me that the Holy Spirit revealed to him that God had a special plan for me—to be a preacher—but first I had to get rid of the sin.[6]

Just like the natives of Malta, the young man assumed that Dravecky's calamity was evidence of some guilt. But, like Paul's snakebite, his cancer was not a result of personal sin. If it was, what kind of God would we be serving?

> The issue is not *our* character but the character of God.
>
> Is God the kind of God who gives people tumors when they sin? Does he dole out diseases when we fail him? Say, maybe, cataracts when we lust or hardening of the arteries when we hate. Does he punish us with leukemia and muscular dystrophy and blindness?
>
> The [disciples] thought so. When they came across a blind man, they asked Jesus, "Who sinned, this man or his parents, that he was born blind?" Jesus responded by saying "neither," and then proceeded to heal the man.[7]

Psalm 103:10–14 describes that divine healing touch, portraying God's infinite compassion toward us in our sin. Take a moment right now to read those verses.

If you're suffering like Dave Dravecky or the apostle Paul and someone has thrown you a curve, what comfort do these verses give you?

_____

_____

_____

6. Dave and Jan Dravecky, with Ken Gire, *When You Can't Come Back* (Grand Rapids, Mich.: Zondervan Publishing House; San Francisco, Calif.: HarperSanFrancisco, 1992), p. 72.

7. Dravecky, Dravecky, and Gire, *When You Can't Come Back*, p. 72.

Thinking about the image of God portrayed in Psalm 103, Dravecky adds:

> Is that the picture of a father who takes a belt to his children when they spill their milk or wet their pants? Is that the picture of a God who gives people cancer when they sin? I don't think so.
>
> I didn't get angry with the man. I felt sad that he was carrying around such a distorted picture of God. And I wondered how that picture would get him through life when one day he would have to walk through his own valley of suffering.[8]

Take a moment to reach into your mental wallet and examine the picture of God you carry with you. Is it a distorted image like the one that young man held? Or does it resemble the God pictured in Psalm 103?

 Living Insights

"What do you do for fun?" asked the wise doctor.

The visibly exhausted young mother had come to see him for physical, not social, advice. Surprised by his question, she glanced around the examining room and stammered, "Wha, what do you mean?"

"Fun . . . you know, hobbies, sports, recreation. Don't you do anything just to relax and enjoy yourself?"

She began, "Well, I . . . no that was years ago. Oh, I know, I . . . no, not anymore." Suddenly it occurred to her that, with the kids, work, the house, church, and all the other demands on her time, she didn't do anything for fun. Nothing.

Do you feel like this young mother? If so, somewhere in your life you need a Malta, an island of refuge, a place to hide from life's storms and heal.

---

8. Dravecky, Dravecky, and Gire, *When You Can't Come Back*, p. 73.

If you had three hours per week of uninterrupted time for fun, restoration, and refreshment, how would you spend it? Would you take dancing lessons? Ride a bike? Play a sport? Learn how to paint? What would you do?

_____

_____

The problem is, most of us feel these kinds of activities are selfish and un-Christian. Free time should be spent calling a needy friend, working at church, or reading our Bibles. We feel irresponsible if we take time to be alone or relax with friends. But such therapeutic time is crucial for our health.

Because relaxation is so valuable and often so ignored, we must plan to make it happen or it will easily suffer shipwreck because of busy schedules. Where in your week can you carve out a few hours for restorative fun? What details do you need to work out? Pray for God's help in finding your Malta, and then make specific plans to spend some time there.

_____

_____

_____

_____

_____

Chapter 12
POWER, POWER . . .
WE'VE GOT THE POWER!
Selected Scriptures

"But you shall receive power when the Holy Spirit
has come upon you." (Acts 1:8a)

As we saw earlier, in chapter 2, the power Jesus promised His
disciples manifested itself in some startling ways on that day
of Pentecost. Remember their remarkable preaching, invincible
courage, unshakable confidence, and miraculous healings? Those
twelve men suddenly shot into public awareness like comets burning
with the incandescence of divine power.

"And then," some of you may be thinking, "there's me; my
life—my ordinary, uneventful, down-to-earth existence."

Have you ever done that—compared yourself to the apostles
and come up short on the supernatural side of displaying the Spirit's
power? Many of us have. So we begin to wonder whether we even
have the Spirit or whether perhaps we've missed some secret key
for unlocking His power.

But are our lives really all that common and lacking in power?
Or have we mistakenly bought into the misconception that unless
we're experiencing one miracle after another we're not filled with
the Spirit? Think about it. Is that what Jesus really promised—a
miracle a moment—when He said we would receive power when
the Spirit came?

Not even the disciples lived that kind of life. Look past the day
of Pentecost, and you'll find that they experienced disappointments
and hardships just like the rest of us. Or consider the apostle Paul—
whipped, beaten, stoned, and hounded throughout Palestine and
Asia. Power was displayed in his ministry, not because he led a
charmed life from one miraculous mountaintop to the next, but
because he glorified Christ in the deepest trenches of life's difficulties. Now that's power. And we must never forget that it can burn
brightly in each of us whether or not we ever perform a miracle.

Could it be that the power demonstrated in your life isn't as
lackluster as you think? To convince you of this, take your eyes off
the miraculous events surrounding Pentecost and join us as we focus

on those evidences of Spirit-filled power that you and I can experience every day.

Understanding First Things First

To begin, let's review the two basic truths from which the Spirit's power flows.

I Am a Christian Because . . .

The fundamental necessity for receiving the power Jesus promised in Acts 1:8 is salvation. And what must we do to be saved? A Roman jailer once asked this very question of Paul, who answered, "Believe in the Lord Jesus, and you shall be saved" (Acts 16:30–31a). This same truth is also confirmed by the apostle John:

> And the witness is this, that God has given us eternal life, and this life is in His Son. He who has the Son has the life; he who does not have the Son of God does not have the life. (1 John 5:11–12)

Notice that John doesn't say we have eternal life because we attend church or were baptized or give away lots of money. The issue is whether or not we have Jesus, God's free gift. As Paul wrote in Ephesians 2:8–9:

> For by grace you have been saved through faith; and that not of yourselves, it is the gift of God; not as a result of works, that no one should boast.

One way of affirming our salvation would be to say, "I am a Christian because . . . I am rightly related to the Son of God, the Lord Jesus Christ." At the moment we become rightly related to Him through faith, many exciting things occur—not the least of which is that we're *given* the Holy Spirit for the rest of our lives!

Note this well: nowhere in Scripture are we commanded to pray to receive the Spirit, be baptized by Him, be regenerated by Him, or be sealed by Him. Why? Because all these things occurred the moment we trusted Christ for salvation (see 1 Cor. 12:12–13; Eph. 1:13–14; Titus 3:5–7). What we are commanded to do, however, once we are Christians, is to "be filled with the Spirit" (Eph. 5:18). So let's shift our attention to this truth that governs the release of the Spirit's power in our lives.

97

I Am Filled with the Spirit When . . .

Because we devoted all of chapter 4 to this, we needn't go into much detail here. Suffice it to say that we are filled with the Spirit when . . . we allow Him full control of our lives, keep short accounts with Him about sin, and walk in complete dependence upon Him.

The results of that kind of attitude and life are numerous and deeply intimate in our Christian experience—but not necessarily (or routinely) ecstatic or miraculous in nature. The Christian life is not a day-to-day, moment-by-moment hyper-spiritualism marked by power visions, power healings, power evangelism, power encounters, power everything! Certainly, the Spirit brings a dynamic and depth we would not have otherwise. And yes, He can and does cause miracles to occur on occasion. But they are the exception, not the rule. Let's not twist the reality of His presence into some kind of fantasyland version of Christianity. We need to keep ourselves firmly rooted in the reality presented in the Scriptures. And what is that, exactly? I'm glad you asked.

Understanding the Continual, Normal Evidences of the Spirit's Empowering

For a more realistic and comprehensive appraisal of the Spirit's empowering, consider, first of all, these evidences that apply to all Christians.

As a Christian, . . .

- I am in Christ. I live in Him and He lives in me.

- I am able to live above sin's dominating control.

- I have immediate access to the Father through prayer.

- I can understand the Scriptures.

- I am able to forgive—and should forgive—whoever wrongs me.

- I have the capacity to bear fruit daily, continually, routinely.

- I possess at least one (sometimes more than one) spiritual gift.

- I worship with joy and with purpose.

- I have a faith to share with others.

- I love and need other people.

- I am able to obey the teaching of the Word of God.

- I continue to learn and grow toward maturity.

- I can endure suffering and hardship without losing heart.

- I depend and trust in my Lord for daily strength and provisions.

- I can know God's will.

- I now live in anticipation of Christ's return.

- I have the assurance of heaven after I die.

None of what we've just listed is true of the unsaved. Only those in a right relationship with Jesus Christ possess these unique blessings. They are ours to claim every day. And though none of them are what we would call miraculous, they are truly remarkable.

It is in the outworking of these evidences in our lives that we experience most of our Christianity, not in the rare stratosphere of the supernatural. And until we realize this and recognize the treasure we have, we'll be disappointed, frustrated, and always looking for more . . . while missing the abundant life Christ has spread before us.

To continue, consider now a brief sampling of the evidences for the Spirit-filled life.

When Spirit-filled, . . .

- I am surrounded by the Spirit's omnipotent shield of protection, continually and routinely.

- I have an "inner dynamic" to handle life's pressures.

- I am able to be joyful regardless of the circumstances.

- I have the capacity to grasp the deep things of God which He discloses to us in His Book.

- I am able to maintain a positive attitude of unselfishness, servanthood, and humility.

- I have a keen sense of discernment; I can sense evil.

- I am able to love and be loved in return.

- I can be vulnerable and open.

- I can rely on the Spirit to intercede for me when I don't know how to pray as I should.

- I am enabled to stand alone with confidence.

- I experience inner assurance regarding decisions as well as right and wrong.

- I have an "internal filter system."

- I can actually live worry-free.

- I am able to minister to others through my spiritual gift(s).

- I am never truly alone.

- I have an intimate, abiding "Abba relationship" with the living God.

Again, notice that none of what has been listed is exceptional or phenomenal. Rather, each is routinely available to anyone who humbly seeks the Spirit-filled way of living. It is these marvelous truths and many others like them that shine through our lives with the incandescence of divine power. Now do you see? Your life is not so common or ordinary after all!

Admitting Occasional Exceptional Experiences

In attempting to show that the Spirit's power is displayed in all Christians in a myriad of ways, most of which are not miraculous, we are in danger of leaving the wrong impression about miracles altogether. Are we saying that Christians should never experience the miraculous? Or suggesting that anything supernatural be viewed with skepticism, as if it never comes from God's Spirit? No and no! And to help safeguard against such a misunderstanding, here are three important conclusions to balance our perspective.

1. *God is the God of the miraculous* . . . therefore, miracles do occur. The fact that they happen, however, is no proof that they're to happen all the time in every believer's life. Nothing in Scripture would support such a huge leap of logic. Miracles are the exception, not the norm.

2. *God is the God of the supernatural* . . . therefore, supernatural phenomena occur. Again, the Scripture suggests that they are occasional, not routine. Ask God for discernment and wisdom in evaluating any exceptional experiences you may encounter.

3. *God is the God of the mysterious* . . . therefore, mysterious things occur that we can't explain. The Lord is infinite in nature and His ways are higher than ours (Isa. 55:8–9). Limited as we are by our finite humanity, we cannot always comprehend His purpose and plan. Yet, again, miraculous mysteries play only a small part of our experience. God is not playing cat and mouse with us. He has revealed Himself through His Son and His Word to remove the veil of mystery between us so that we can love and obey Him.

 ## Living Insights

As we mentioned in the chapter, the evidences of the Spirit's power that we named represent only a partial list. Can you think of some more? It would be good to exercise your thinking in this area so that you become more personally aware of His power. Use the space provided to brainstorm as many evidences as possible. You might even consider doing this more than once. Come up with all that you can now, and then try again later. This usually frees up the mind to look at something from more than one perspective.

Evidences of Spirit-Filled Power

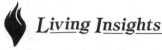 **Living Insights**

In a sincere effort to find deeper intimacy with God, many Christians have reversed the biblical reality of Spirit-filled living and attempted to make the miraculous their normative experience. Everything then becomes a "power encounter." We don't simply pray anymore, we offer power prayers. We don't simply witness, we conduct power evangelism. We also have power healings, power preaching, power miracles, and power revelations, just to name a few.

Power is one of the "in" terms of our times, and it has been overused and abused by many Christians. Be careful, Christian friend, not to measure your intimacy with God by miraculous experiences. To do so will only result in your setting up expectations that will let you down and lead you astray. Let the Spirit wield the power, not you. You stay focused on being faithful. Intimacy with God flourishes in obedience, that is where your love for Him is brought to maturity.

Remember these Spirit-inspired words from the apostle John:

- "If you love Me, you will keep My commandments. . . . He who has My commandments and keeps them, he it is who loves Me; and he who loves Me shall be loved by My Father, and I will love him, and will disclose Myself to him." (John 14:15, 21)

- And by this we know that we have come to know Him, if we keep His commandments. The one who says, "I have come to know Him," and does not keep His commandments, is a liar, and the truth is not in him; but whoever keeps His word, in him the love of God has truly been perfected. By this we know that we are in Him: the one who says he abides in Him ought himself to walk in the same manner as He walked. (1 John 2:3–6)

- For this is the love of God, that we keep His commandments; and His commandments are not burdensome. (1 John 5:3)

- And this is love, that we walk according to His commandments. This is the commandment, just as you have heard from the beginning, that you should walk in it. (2 John 6)

Chapter 13

IS THAT ALL THERE IS TO THE SPIRIT'S MINISTRY?

Selected Scriptures

From the beginning of our study, our emphasis has been on developing a more intimate and practical understanding of the Holy Spirit. So we've purposely avoided some of the more esoteric, theological fine print and focused instead on the personal aspects of His ministry: things like His filling, anointing, and empowering, just to name a few. We hope these and many other discoveries have sparked a desire in you to continue searching the Scriptures to learn more about God's wonderful Spirit.

As the end of our journey nears, an important question must be raised that is relevant to us all: Have we reached the end of the Spirit's era? Or, to put it in the simple words of a child, "Dear God, How come you did all those miracles in the old days and don't do any now?"[1]

You see, even a child realizes that times are different today from what they were when Moses or Jesus or even the apostles were alive. We don't see fire falling from heaven, seas parting, fish and loaves multiplying, or other miracles of healing or raising the dead like there once were. Certainly, miracles still occur, but they don't seem to flow like they used to. What's happened? Has the Spirit's work dwindled to an end? Have His presence and power ceased?

Absolutely not! Remember what Jesus told the disciples about the Spirit?

> "I will ask the Father, and He will give you another Helper, that *He may be with you forever*; that is the Spirit of truth, whom the world cannot receive, because it does not behold Him or know Him, but you know Him because He abides with you, and will be in you." (John 14:16–17, emphasis added)

The one constant we can always count on is the Spirit Himself.

---

1. Stuart Hample and Eric Marshall, comps., "Seymour," *Children's Letters to God* (New York, N.Y.: Workman Publishing, 1991), p. 44.

His presence in us will never change. That He doesn't perform miracles with the same frequency He did during the apostolic era doesn't mean He's abandoned us to fend for ourselves. It simply means that His method of ministry has changed from what it used to be in the early church.

What Has Ceased . . . What Continues?

Perhaps if we take a look at a few verses tucked away in 1 Corinthians 13, we'll gain a better understanding of why the Spirit's work is different today.

> If there are gifts of prophecy, they will be done away; if there are tongues, they will cease; if there is knowledge, it will be done away. For we know in part, and we prophesy in part; but when the perfect comes, the partial will be done away. When I was a child, I used to speak as a child, think as a child, reason as a child; when I became a man, I did away with childish things. (vv. 13:8b–11)

As in life, the natural progression of growth toward maturity is also reflected in the development of God's church. In its early infancy, before there was a Bible,

> while the church was being built, while the foundation was being laid, [it was necessary] for there to be gifts like prophecy, tongues and apostleship, miracles, healings, and interpretation of tongues, all essential for authenticating the messengers, establishing the church, and propagating the gospel rapidly through the various languages.[2]

This same concept of progression is also hinted at in Ephesians 2.

> So then you are no longer strangers and aliens, but you are fellow citizens with the saints, and are of God's household, having been built upon the foundation of the apostles and prophets, Christ Jesus Himself being the corner stone, in whom the whole building,

2. Charles R. Swindoll, *Flying Closer to the Flame* (Dallas, Tex.: Word Publishing, 1993), chap. 13.

being fitted together is growing into a holy temple
in the Lord; in whom you also are being built together
into a dwelling of God in the Spirit. (vv. 19–22)

Paul describes the church as a great temple whose foundation
was laid by the apostles and prophets. Christ Himself is the corner-
stone upon which "the entire building was lined up. . . . That is,
the apostles and prophets needed to be correctly aligned with
Christ."[3] Consistent with this analogy, the Spirit is continually
building on that foundation to bring God's church to full and complete maturity. According to Charles Ryrie, however, He no longer
uses all the same tools or gifts He once did when the work began.

> There are stages of growth within the present
> imperfect time before Christ's return. After the
> church began, there was a period of immaturity, dur-
> ing which spectacular gifts were needed for growth
> and authentication (Heb. 2:3–4). With the comple-
> tion of the [New Testament] and the growing maturity
> of the church, the need for such gifts disappeared.[4]

In What Way Is the Spirit's Work Still Evident?

If it is true that supernatural gifts have ceased, what aspects of
the Spirit's ministry continue? Obviously, many of His works are
still going on today, as we have seen in the last twelve chapters.
To reaffirm that, here are four undeniable evidences for His ongoing
work among us.

First, *the Bible says that He is still at work in our lives.* Think back
to some of the scriptural truths we've already gleaned from our study.
We know, for example, that the Spirit's work continues because He
lives within us—our bodies are His temple (1 Cor. 6:19–20). Also,
remember Paul's words in Romans 8, where he says that the Spirit
"bears witness with our spirit that we are children of God" (v. 16)?
Add to this 1 John 4:46, "Greater is He who is in you than he who
is in the world," and there can be little doubt that the Spirit is still
working in us today.

---

3. Harold W. Hoehner, "Ephesians," in *The Bible Knowledge Commentary,* New Testament
ed., ed. John F. Walvoord and Roy B. Zuck (Wheaton, Ill.: Scripture Press Publications,
Victor Books, 1983), p. 627.

4. Charles Caldwell Ryrie, *The Ryrie Study Bible* (Chicago, Ill.: Moody Press, 1978), p. 1744.

Second, we know the Spirit is at work because *He is still empowering gifted Christians for ministry.* The apostle Paul provides us with the proof text for this truth.

> Now there are varieties of gifts, but the same Spirit. And there are varieties of ministries, and the same Lord. And there are varieties of effects, but the same God who works all things in all persons. But to each one is given the manifestation of the Spirit for the common good. (1 Cor. 12:4–7)

Every time gifted teachers teach the Word of God, the Spirit is at work. Every time evangelists lead others to Christ, it bears witness to the Spirit's power and presence. Every time we see others show hospitality or mercy, we're given an eloquent and convincing testimony concerning His ongoing ministry among us.

Third, *the Spirit is still restraining lawlessness all around the world* Paul testifies again on behalf of the Spirit:

> For the mystery of lawlessness is already at work; only he who now restrains will do so until he is taken out of the way. And then that lawless one will be revealed whom the Lord will slay with the breath of His mouth and bring to an end by the appearance of His coming. (2 Thess. 2:7–8)

Imagine how chaotic and cruelly evil the world would be if not for the restraining work of the Spirit. The evening news is already saturated with stories that illustrate Paul's fated words in 2 Timothy 3:

> For men will be lovers of self, lovers of money, boastful, arrogant, revilers, disobedient to parents, ungrateful, unholy, unloving, irreconcilable, malicious gossips, without self-control, brutal, haters of good, treacherous, reckless, conceited, lovers of pleasure rather than lovers of God. (vv. 2–4)

Are our times really that bad? There's no denying it. But it will get even worse, unimaginably so, when God removes the controlling, positive influence of His Spirit.

Fourth, *the Spirit is still regenerating the lost.* It is the Spirit who convicts the world of sin, righteousness, and judgment (John 16:8–11). And through this ministry, He acts as a kind of midwife in the spiritual rebirth of every individual who believes in Christ. Remember

Jesus' words?

> "Truly, truly, I say to you, unless one is born again, he cannot see the kingdom of God. . . . That which is born of the flesh is flesh, and that which is born of the Spirit is spirit. Do not marvel that I said to you, 'You must be born again.' The wind blows where it wishes and you hear the sound of it, but do not know where it comes from and where it is going; so is everyone who is born of the Spirit." (John 3:3, 6–8)

The salvation of souls every day all around the world is a constant reminder of the Spirit's work today.

Concluding Checkpoints to Guard against Error

While it is encouraging to know and affirm that the Spirit is still active today, we must also recognize that our selfish natures and Satan are also alive and well. So to help guard ourselves against error, here are five practical guidelines.

1. *Always let your Bible be your guide.* Don't put your Bible on the shelf and simply obey the instructions of others. Read and study God's Word for yourself. Constantly compare the teaching that you're given with the Scriptures, because the worst mistake you could make is to blindly follow someone else. And remember the example of the Jews in Berea, whom Luke described as "noble-minded" because they examined Paul and Silas' teaching "with great eagerness, examining the Scriptures daily, to see whether these things were so" (Acts 17:11).

2. *Be discerning.* Sometimes it pays to be a little skeptical, so keep asking questions. Check out the character of the person teaching. Don't jump into something new without first giving yourself ample time to examine it thoroughly.

3. *Stay balanced.* Guard against extremism. If you find yourself alienating those who are strong and mature in their walk with Christ, put on the brakes, because something is wrong. God is building up His body with contagious Christians, not frightful fanatics.

4. *Seek the counsel of men and women you admire.* If you're feeling unsettled about what you are being taught, talk it over with some mature Christians who are totally outside of the situation. They can listen with an objective ear and provide you with a helpful perspective that, hopefully, will steer you away from any error.

5. *Keep the unity.* The unity of the Spirit is not simply a nice option, it is a command. If something you're doing or believing is becoming divisive—question it! Certainly there are times when it is necessary, painfully so, to take a stand. Just don't allow nitpicking dissensions to become your focus rather than the unity Paul commends in Philippians 2:

> If therefore there is any encouragement in Christ, if there is any consolation of love, if there is any fellowship of the Spirit, if any affection and compassion, make my joy complete by being of the same mind, maintaining the same love, united in spirit, intent on one purpose. (vv. 1–2)

 Living Insights

As well-intentioned as our goal has been to encourage a more intimate understanding between you and the Holy Spirit, most likely some of you are feeling unsettled right now about some of the things we've studied. Perhaps it was the way we applied a verse of Scripture, an observation that was made, or an interpretation. Maybe you're thinking we missed something altogether or, perhaps, added too much to something else. What should you do? Believe everything you've read simply because it's in print by a reputable publisher and author? If you do, then you've already forgotten an important guideline for guarding against error.

Remember what we said? When you're not sure of something, seek the counsel of men and women of the faith whom you respect. In particular, talk to those individuals who are not caught up in your same quandary.

In the space provided, list any concerns, questions, or disagreements you feel need further study for clarification and verification. Then, below that, write down the names of one or two people whom you might approach for help in exploring these issues. Last, we'll leave you as much space as possible to write out the answers you find.

Issues for Further Study

_____

_____

Mentor Help

Answers Found

 **Living Insights**

When it comes to the subject of the Holy Spirit, beware of porcupines. What I mean is, beware of those Christians who are like porcupines because of all their needle-sharp theological points. They love using them to impale others who disagree with their view of the Spirit.

Have you ever had the painful experience of brushing up against someone like that? If you have, you'll probably never forget it. For those of you who haven't and would like to avoid this kind of divisive creature, here are a few tips for spotting the porcupine.

- He's the type who studies the Spirit to gain ammunition for his theological arsenal, not to gain a greater sense of understanding or intimacy.

- She feels close to the Spirit only when she's out there firing away at the supposed fallacies in other people's thinking.

- He has never looked upon the subject of the Spirit as anything but a field of battle.

- She gets excited about the Spirit every time she wins an argument.

The enemy would like nothing more than to keep us sidetracked in arguments and disagreements that breed disunity—especially as it concerns the Spirit.

Could it be that you've been caught up in this kind of porcupine mentality? Take a moment to examine your motive for studying the Holy Spirit. Has it really been to know Him better? Is that what gets you excited? Or is it more to find the faults in other people's faith?

Instead of using our knowledge to add notches to our Bibles, Paul urges us to seek unity and peace on common ground. Consider what he wrote in Romans 14. In fact, take some time to read that chapter right now.

The context may have originally been about whether to continue observing dietary laws and certain feast days, but the broader principles can easily apply to how we handle our differences about the Spirit today. How would verses 4, 10, 13, and 16 affect the way you disagree?

_____

_____

_____

What is Paul's constructive counsel in verses 17 and 19?

_____

_____

How can you better demonstrate these peacemaking words?

_____

_____

_____

_____

I, therefore, the prisoner of the Lord, entreat you to walk in a manner worthy of the calling with which you have been called, with all humility and gentleness, with patience, showing forbearance to one another in love, being diligent to preserve the unity of the Spirit in the bond of peace. (Eph. 4:1–3)

Chapter 14

LET'S JUST PRAISE THE LORD

Psalms 146–150

For those of you who truly want to fly closer to the flame, we have one last flying lesson to offer—soaring on the wings of praise. Practice this spiritual discipline regularly, and you'll develop your wings to fly higher, further, closer to the Lord than you've probably ever flown before.

Afraid of flying so high? Of veering out of control and into uncharted lands? Take heart. With a little basic training from the Psalms, we'll overcome these obstacles so that by the end of the lesson, you'll be ready to take off and fly solo, soaring on the wings of praise.

The Group of Five Psalms

Flight school will be held in the last five chapters of God's hymnbook known as the Psalms. By way of introduction, let's make two general observations.

First, turn to Psalms 146–150 and note the similarity between them. They all begin and end with the same exuberant exhortation—"Praise the Lord!" The actual Hebrew word the psalmist uses is *hallelujah*, which is made up of two terms: *halal*, meaning "to boast," and *Yah*, the three-letter word representing Jehovah in the Hebrew Bible. "Boast in Jehovah!" the psalmist declares again and again in a rousing hallelujah chorus that closes the book.

Second, the tone throughout these psalms, though realistic, is joyful. Not one morbid, negative, or pessimistic thought is expressed. In fact, resonating through the fifty-nine verses of these five hymns are forty-four references to praise. Now this doesn't mean the writer walked around with his head in the clouds, unaware of suffering and pain. It simply means that when we lift up our eyes to focus on God's goodness and greatness, our hearts are lifted up as well to experience the beautiful harmony of praise and joy.

Using a simple outline to make things easier to remember, let's

---

This message was not a part of the original series but is compatible with it.

now briefly examine each psalm in this section to learn the basics for flying closer through praise.

Psalm 146—When We Praise Him

> Praise the Lord!
> Praise the Lord, O my soul! (v. 1)

Pause for just a moment to think about the psalmist's choice of words here. Notice he doesn't say to praise the Lord with our lips but to praise Him with our souls. True praise is not lip service; it is much more profound than that. It comes from deep within our hearts, from our innermost being. And when does the psalmist himself practice such heartfelt praise?

> I will praise the Lord while I live;
> I will sing praises to my God while I have my being.
> (v. 2)

For some people, praise is something they think of doing only after they die and are assigned a cloud and a harp. But that's simply the stuff of cartoons. Reality is glorifying God *now*, while we live and have our being.

"But what if I don't have anything to praise Him about?" some of you may be thinking. "What if my world has collapsed in a tangled mess of chaos and pain?" Then you, my friend, are exactly the person the psalmist had in mind when he wrote this song. He's speaking to those who need "help" and "hope" (v. 5); who are oppressed, hungry, imprisoned, afflicted, a stranger, or lonely (vv. 7–9). It's precisely during those hurting times that we need to keep our focus on the Lord and on His goodness toward us. And the praise which arises out of the ashes of our grief will lead us to a place of refuge and comfort in His arms.

Psalm 147—Whom Do We Praise?

This next psalm reminds us that the Lord is to be the focus of our worshipful adoration, not ourselves, others, or human accomplishments (v. 1a). "It is good to sing praises to our God," verse 1 continues, "For it is pleasant and praise is becoming" (v. 1b). Why? Because . . .

> He builds up (v. 2)
> He gathers the outcasts (v. 2)

113

He heals the brokenhearted (v. 3a)
He binds up wounds (v. 3b)
He is abundantly strong and infinitely understanding
    (v. 5)
He is supportive (v. 6)

Despite the overwhelming evidence of these and many other gracious truths concerning the Lord, it is still ourselves, our plans, and our works that receive the most attention and praise. Why not turn that around? Why not begin today making our praise of Him a priority?

Remember, God does not delight in the strong or the mighty whose focus is on themselves (vv. 10–11). His pleasure comes from those who revere Him with awe and worship. So,

Sing to the Lord with thanksgiving;
Sing praises to our God on the lyre. (v. 7)

Psalm 148—Where We Praise Him

The psalmist next calls on all of creation to join in a glorious paean to the Creator. First he turns to the sky, beckoning its inhabitants to join his hallelujah chorus—angels, sun, moon, stars, and highest heavens (vv. 1–6).

His attention then shifts to the earth, where again he recruits creatures and creation alike to sing out God's glory.

Praise the Lord from the earth,
Sea monsters and all deeps;
Fire and hail, snow and clouds;
Stormy wind, fulfilling His word;
Mountains and all hills;
Fruit trees and all cedars;
Beasts and all cattle;
Creeping things and winged fowl;
Kings of the earth and all peoples;
Princes and all judges of the earth;
Both young men and virgins;
Old men and children. (vv. 7–12)

The inescapable message behind the psalmist's tour of the heavens and earth is that praise is universal. All creation, including you and me, is encouraged to lift up its voice in unrestrained adoration wherever we may find ourselves.

Psalm 149—How We Praise Him

Moving on, the psalmist turns our attention to that phase of our training that deals with technique, the how-to's of praise.

> Praise the Lord!
> Sing to the Lord a new song,
> And His praise in the congregation of the godly
>   ones. (v. 1)

The first method highlighted here is singing. "But I don't know how to sing. My voice is awful!" How many of you are thinking this right now? It's the excuse many of us give for not singing—not in church, not in small groups, not alone, not anywhere, anytime.

But do you see what's happening when we do this? We're focusing on ourselves instead of the Lord. *I* can't sing; *I'm* embarrassed; what will the others think of *me*? Not only does this kind of self-absorption rob the Lord of His rightful praise, it also robs the church of her strength and witness. Whether you sound like an angel or an alley cat, "sing to the Lord a new song"! It's the harmony of your heart that He listens to, not your vocal chords.

If you think this first assignment is difficult, wait till you read verse 3!

> Let them praise His name with dancing;
> Let them sing praises to Him with timbrel and lyre.

When was the last time you praised God with dancing? The very idea has become so foreign to our culture and time that we rarely, if ever, see such a thing. But have you ever been so enthused about the Lord that you felt like you just couldn't sit still? David had an experience like that. When the ark of the Lord was finally being brought to Jerusalem, he literally danced before the Lord with all his might (2 Sam. 6:14–15). David—the great king and warrior—was leaping and dancing with joy! Certainly, we're not to practice this to draw attention to ourselves or disrupt other people's worship, but it just may be the best way you have, on occasion, of expressing more fully your praise to Him.

Finally, praise is not only to be sung and expressed physically, it is to be spoken.

> Let the high praises of God be in their mouth.
> (Ps. 149:6a)

Here's a helpful formula to encourage the practice of worshiping God with your words: praise Him for His work and His Word, His Person and His plan. Do this, and you will have an unlimited supply of things to praise Him about.

Psalm 150—Why We Praise Him

The last course to complete our basic training touches on motivation—why practice the spiritual discipline of praise? Our instructor gives us two important reasons in verse 2.

> Praise Him for His mighty deeds;
> Praise Him according to His excellent greatness.

Look a little closer at what the psalmist's words reveal. We express praise, first, because of what God does—"mighty deeds"; and, second, because of what He is—"excellent greatness." Who He is and what He does are what empower our praise. They are what fill our minds, capture our imaginations, and fire our hearts to fly closer to the flame.

School is out. Have fun soaring!

 Living Insights STUDY ONE

These past fourteen chapters have been an incredible journey that's taken many of you through some unfamiliar yet intriguing terrain. As you complete the trip with these next two Living Insights, it is our sincere hope that the reward you will take with you for the rest of your life will be a much deeper, richer relationship with the Spirit.

As you may recall, we began this study on the Spirit by asking you to make a verbal sketch of how you honestly perceived the Spirit. Take a moment now to compose a second sketch, this time describing the Spirit as you've come to know Him through this study. After you do that, compare the two and note the differences you see in the space provided. It will give you a clear glimpse into the reward that you've reaped from the work that you've sown.

Sketch

Comparative Differences

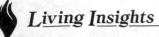 **Living Insights**

In keeping with the theme of Psalms 146–150, listen to these words from Charles Spurgeon as he reminds us of our need to praise God's "good Spirit" (Neh. 9:20).

> Common, too common is the sin of forgetting the Holy Spirit. This is folly and ingratitude. He deserves well at our hands, for He is good, supremely good. As God, He is *good essentially*. He shares in the threefold ascription of Holy, holy, holy, which ascends to the Triune Jehovah. Unmixed purity, and truth, and grace is He. He is *good benevolently*, tenderly bearing with our waywardness, striving with our rebellious wills; quickening us from our death in sin, and then training us for the skies as a loving nurse fosters her child. . . . He is *good operatively*. All His works are good in the most eminent degree: He suggests good thoughts, prompts good actions, reveals good truths, applies good promises, assists in good attainments, and leads to good results. There is no spiritual good in all the world of which He is not the author and sustainer. . . . They who yield to His influences become good, they who obey His impulses do good, they who live under His power receive good. . . . Let us revere His person, and adore Him as God over all, blessed for ever; let us own His power, and our need of Him by waiting upon Him in all our holy enterprises; let us hourly seek His aid, and never grieve Him; and let us speak to His praise whenever the occasion occurs.[1]

Right now is such an occasion. As a fitting closing, be still before Him and offer up praise for the good things He has revealed about Himself to you through this guide.

1Charles H. Spurgeon, *Morning and Evening: Daily Readings* (McLean, Va.: MacDonald Publishing Co., n.d.), p. 95.

FLYING CLOSER TO THE FLAME

Guidance, comfort, power, conviction . . . what believer does not long, at one time or another, for the indispensable ministry of the Holy Spirit? His indwelling at the time of salvation is only the beginning of a lifelong journey of faith under His influence. The following volumes complement this study guide's theme of intimacy with the Spirit; each has been selected for its spiritual sensitivity and careful scholarship.

The Mystery of the Holy Spirit—"This book is written for those who desire a deeper spiritual life, a result that cannot happen apart from the Spirit, the One who sanctifies," writes renowned theologian R. C. Sproul. His approach to doctrine is personable and easy to read; his careful presentation of the sometimes complex or controversial questions about the Holy Spirit makes this book an asset to any person seeking to "draw closer to the flame."

Baptism and Fullness: The Work of the Holy Spirit Today—This short book by John Stott (only 120 pages) contains one of the best and most thoroughly researched definitions of the filling of the Spirit. Stott divides his study into four major areas: the promise of the Spirit, the fullness of the Spirit, the fruit and the gifts of the Spirit.

Powerlines—Don't let this book's subtitle, *What Great Evangelicals Believed about the Holy Spirit 1850–1930*, scare you off! Leona Frances Choy's interview format introduces you to twenty-four godly Christian leaders, including D. L. Moody, Oswald Chambers, and Hannah Whitehall Smith. Each leader's experiences with and understanding of the Spirit are intimately showcased in excerpts from their writings.

ORDER FORM

This special offer expires January 31, 1994.

Title	California	U.S.	Canada	Quantity	Amount
The Mystery of the Holy Spirit (MHSHB) (hardcover)	$14.17	$13.15	$17.75	_____	$_____
Baptism and Fullness (BAPPB) (softcover)	7.65	7.10	9.60	_____	_____
Powerlines (PWRPB) (softcover)	14.17	13.15	17.75	_____	_____

Subtotal $_____

For faster shipping, United States residents can add 10 percent for first-class shipping and handling. _____

Contribution to the Insight for Living radio ministry. _____

All contributions are tax-deductible.

Total Amount Enclosed $_____

Check or money order should be made payable to Insight for Living.

These prices have been discounted 10 percent from retail price. All prices include applicable taxes and shipping costs.

Credit card purchases: ❑ Visa ❑ MasterCard ❑ Discover Card

Expiration Date _____ Number _____

Signature _____
We cannot process your credit card purchase without your signature.

For credit card orders, you are welcome to use one of our toll-free numbers between the hours of 7:00 A.M. and 4:30 P.M., Pacific time, Monday through Friday, or our FAX numbers. The numbers to use from anywhere in the United States are **1-800-772-8888** or FAX (714) 575-5496. To order from Canada, call our Vancouver office using **1-800-663-7639** or FAX (604) 596-2975. Vancouver residents, call (604) 596-2910.

Name _____

Address _____

City _____

State/Province _____ Zip/Postal Code _____

Country _____

Telephone (_____) _____ Radio Station ____ ____ ____ ____
If questions arise concerning your order, we may need to contact you.

Insight for Living • Post Office Box 69000, Anaheim, CA 92817-0900
Insight for Living Ministries • Post Office Box 2510, Vancouver, BC, Canada V6B 3W7
Please allow four to six weeks for delivery.

BOOKS FOR
PROBING FURTHER

For further instruction on how to fly closer to the Holy Spirit's flame, here are some excellent resources.

Choy, Leona Frances. *Powerlines: What Great Evangelicals Believed about the Holy Spirit 1850–1930.* Camp Hill, Pa.: Christian Publications, 1990.

Ryrie, Charles Caldwell. *The Holy Spirit.* Chicago, Ill.: Moody Press, 1965.

Sproul, R. C. *The Mystery of the Holy Spirit.* Wheaton, Ill.: Tyndale House Publishers, 1990.

Stott, John R. W. *Baptism and Fullness: The Work of the Holy Spirit Today.* 2d ed. Downers Grove, Ill.: InterVarsity Press, 1979.

Swindoll, Charles R. *Flying Closer to the Flame: A Passion for the Holy Spirit.* Dallas, Tex.: Word Publishing, 1993.

All of the books listed above are recommended reading; however, some may be out of print and available only through a library. For books currently available, please contact your local Christian bookstore. Works by Charles R. Swindoll are available through Insight for Living. IFL also offers some books by other authors— please note the Ordering Information that follows and contact the office which serves you.

ACKNOWLEDGMENTS

Insight for Living is grateful to the sources listed below for permission to use their material.

Fulghum, Robert. *It Was on Fire When I Lay Down on It*. New York, N.Y.: Villard Books, 1989. Used by permission of Random House, Inc., New York, and by HarperCollins Publishers, Inc., England.

Stott, John R. W. *Baptism and Fullness: The Work of the Holy Spirit Today*. 2d ed. ©1975, InterVarsity Press, Leicester, England. Used by permission of InterVarsity Press, Post Office Box 1400, Downers Grove, Illinois 60515.

Swindoll, Charles R. *Flying Closer to the Flame: A Passion for the Holy Spirit*. Dallas, Tex.: Word Publishing, 1993. Used by permission.

ORDERING INFORMATION

Cassette Tapes and Study Guide

This Bible study guide was designed to be used independently or in conjunction with the broadcast of Chuck Swindoll's taped messages on the topic listed below. If you would like to order cassette tapes or further copies of this study guide, please see the information given below and the Order Forms provided at the end of this guide.

FLYING CLOSER TO THE FLAME

Let's face it—many of us simply do not understand the Holy Spirit. We feel awkward relating to Him. We don't know what to say or feel or how to act. The bizarre behavior He often gets credited for makes us nervous, so we treat Him like an uninvited guest in the Trinity. We keep Him at arm's length with stiff, dry doctrines. We warily back away instead of warmly drawing near. Like the proverbial moth and flame, we're not sure how close we can fly without burning our wings. We are fascinated by the light, but also frightened by the heat.

If this describes you, let us help you fly past some of your fears into closer intimacy with Him. Is it risky? Perhaps. But you'll never know the joy of His light or the warmth of His heat unless you dare to draw near, dare to fly closer to the Flame.

		Calif.*	U.S.	B.C.*	Canada*
FCF CS	Cassette series, includes album cover	$45.63	$42.55	$54.85	$51.25
FCF 1–7	Individual cassettes, includes messages A and B	6.76	6.30	8.95	8.50
FCF SG	Study guide	5.31	4.95	6.50	6.50

*These prices already include the following charges: for delivery in **California**, applicable sales tax; **Canada**, 7% GST and 7% postage and handling (on tapes only); **British Columbia**, 7% GST, 6% British Columbia sales tax (on tapes only), and 7% postage and handling (on tapes only). **The prices are subject to change without notice.**

FCF   1-A: *Let's Get Reacquainted with the Spirit*—Selected Scriptures
          B: *The Main Agenda of God's Spirit: Transformation*
          —Selected Scriptures

FCF   2-A: *My Sin . . . and "The Things of the Spirit"*—Romans 8
          B: *Is the Spirit's Filling That Big a Deal?*—Selected Scriptures

FCF   3-A: *The Spirit Who Surprises*—1 Corinthians 2:1–13

B: *Draw Me Nearer . . . Nearer*—Selected Scriptures

FCF   4-A: *Those Unidentified Inner Promptings*— Selected Scriptures
      B: *The Spirit and Our Emotions*—Selected Scriptures

FCF   5-A: *Thinking Theologically about Sickness and Healing*—
           Selected Scriptures
      B: *A Biblical Case for Healing*—James 5:13–16

FCF   6-A: *When the Spirit Brings a Slow Recovery*—Acts 28:1–10
      B: *Power, Power . . . We've Got the Power!*—
           Selected Scriptures

FCF   7-A: *Is That All There Is to the Spirit's Ministry?*—
           Selected Scriptures
      B: *Let's Just Praise the Lord*—Psalms 146–150

How to Order by Mail

Simply mark on the order form whether you want the series or individual tapes. Mail the form with your payment to the appropriate address listed below. We will process your order as promptly as we can.

United States: Mail your order to the Ordering Services Department at Insight for Living, Post Office Box 69000, Anaheim, California 92817-0900. If you wish your order to be shipped first-class for faster delivery, add 10 percent of the total order amount. Otherwise, please allow four to six weeks for delivery by fourth-class mail. We accept payment by personal check, money order, or credit card. Unfortunately, we are unable to offer invoicing or COD orders.

Note: To cover processing and handling, there is a $10 fee for *any* returned check.

Canada: Mail your order to Insight for Living Ministries, Post Office Box 2510, Vancouver, British Columbia V6B 3W7. Allow approximately four weeks for delivery. We accept payment by personal check, money order, or credit card. Unfortunately, we are unable to offer invoicing or COD orders.

Australia, New Zealand, or Papua New Guinea: Mail your order to Insight for Living, Inc., GPO Box 2823 EE, Melbourne, Victoria 3001, Australia. Please allow six to ten weeks for delivery by surface mail. If you would like your order sent airmail, the delivery time may be reduced. Using the United States price as a base, add postage costs—surface or airmail— to the amount of your order. Please use the chart that follows to determine correct postage. Due to fluctuating currency rates, we can accept only personal checks made payable in United States funds, international money orders, or credit cards in payment for materials.

Overseas: Other overseas residents should mail their orders to our United States office. Please allow six to ten weeks for delivery by surface mail. If you would like your order sent airmail, the delivery time may be reduced. Using the United States price as a base, add postage costs— surface or airmail—to the amount of your order. Please use the chart that follows to determine correct postage. Due to fluctuating currency rates, we can accept only personal checks made payable in United States funds, international money orders, or credit cards in payment for materials.

Type of Postage	Postage Cost
Surface	10% of total order
Airmail	25% of total order

For Faster Service, Order by Telephone or FAX

For credit card orders, you are welcome to use one of our toll-free numbers between the hours of 7:00 A.M. and 4:30 P.M., Pacific time, Monday through Friday, or our FAX numbers. The numbers to use from anywhere in the United States are **1-800-772-8888** or FAX (714) 575-5496. To order from Canada, call our Vancouver office using **1-800-663-7639** or FAX (604) 596-2975. Vancouver residents, call (604) 596-2910. Australian residents should phone (03) 872-4606. From other international locations, call our Ordering Services Department at (714) 575-5000 in the United States.

Our Guarantee

Your complete satisfaction is our top priority here at Insight for Living. If you're not completely satisfied with anything you order, please return it for full credit, a refund, or a replacement, as you prefer.

Insight for Living Catalog

Request a free copy of the Insight for Living catalog of books, tapes, and study guides by calling **1-800-772-8888** in the United States or **1-800-663-7639** in Canada.

Order Form

FCF CS represents the entire *Flying Closer to the Flame* series in a special album cover, while FCF 1–7 are the individual tapes included in the series. FCF SG represents this study guide, should you desire to order additional copies.

Item	Calif.*	Unit Price U.S.	B.C.*	Canada*	Quantity	Amount
FCF CS	$45.63	$42.55	$54.85	$51.25		$
FCF 1	6.76	6.30	8.95	8.50		
FCF 2	6.76	6.30	8.95	8.50		
FCF 3	6.76	6.30	8.95	8.50		
FCF 4	6.76	6.30	8.95	8.50		
FCF 5	6.76	6.30	8.95	8.50		
FCF 6	6.76	6.30	8.95	8.50		
FCF 7	6.76	6.30	8.95	8.50		
FCF SG	5.31	4.95	6.50	6.50		
					Subtotal	
		Overseas Residents *Pay U.S. price plus 10% surface postage or 25% airmail. Also, see "How to Order by Mail."*				
		U.S. First-Class Shipping *For faster delivery, add 10% for postage and handling.*				
		Gift to Insight for Living *Tax-deductible in the United States and Canada.*				
		Total Amount Due *Please do not send cash.*				$

If there is a balance: ☐ Apply it as a donation ☐ Please refund
*These prices already include applicable taxes and shipping costs.

Payment by: ☐ Check or money order payable to Insight for Living ☐ Credit card

(Circle one): Visa MasterCard Discover Card Number_____

Expiration Date_____ Signature_____
<small>We cannot process your credit card purchase without your signature.</small>

Name_____

Address_____

City_____ State/Province_____

Zip/Postal Code_____ Country_____

Telephone (___)_____ Radio Station___ ___ ___ ___
If questions arise concerning your order, we may need to contact you.

Mail this order form to the Ordering Services Department at one of these addresses:
Insight for Living, Post Office Box 69000, Anaheim, CA 92817-0900
Insight for Living Ministries, Post Office Box 2510, Vancouver, BC, Canada V6B 3W7
Insight for Living, Inc., GPO Box 2823 EE, Melbourne, VIC 3001, Australia

Order Form

FCF CS represents the entire *Flying Closer to the Flame* series in a special album cover, while FCF 1–7 are the individual tapes included in the series. FCF SG represents this study guide, should you desire to order additional copies.

Item	Calif.*	Unit Price U.S.	B.C.*	Canada*	Quantity	Amount
FCF CS	$45.63	$42.55	$54.85	$51.25		$
FCF 1	6.76	6.30	8.95	8.50		
FCF 2	6.76	6.30	8.95	8.50		
FCF 3	6.76	6.30	8.95	8.50		
FCF 4	6.76	6.30	8.95	8.50		
FCF 5	6.76	6.30	8.95	8.50		
FCF 6	6.76	6.30	8.95	8.50		
FCF 7	6.76	6.30	8.95	8.50		
FCF SG	5.31	4.95	6.50	6.50		
					Subtotal	
	Overseas Residents *Pay U.S. price plus 10% surface postage or 25% airmail. Also, see "How to Order by Mail."*					
	U.S. First-Class Shipping *For faster delivery, add 10% for postage and handling.*					
	Gift to Insight for Living *Tax-deductible in the United States and Canada.*					
	Total Amount Due *Please do not send cash.*					$

If there is a balance: ❏ Apply it as a donation ❏ Please refund
*These prices already include applicable taxes and shipping costs.

Payment by: ❏ Check or money order payable to Insight for Living ❏ Credit card

(Circle one): Visa   MasterCard   Discover Card   Number _____

Expiration Date _____   Signature _____

We cannot process your credit card purchase without your signature.

Name _____

Address _____

City _____ State/Province _____

Zip/Postal Code _____   Country _____

Telephone (__) _____   Radio Station ____ ____ ____ ____

If questions arise concerning your order, we may need to contact you.

Mail this order form to the Ordering Services Department at one of these addresses:
Insight for Living, Post Office Box 69000, Anaheim, CA 92817-0900
Insight for Living Ministries, Post Office Box 2510, Vancouver, BC, Canada V6B 3W7
Insight for Living, Inc., GPO Box 2823 EE, Melbourne, VIC 3001, Australia

Order Form

FCF CS represents the entire *Flying Closer to the Flame* series in a special album cover, while FCF 1–7 are the individual tapes included in the series. FCF SG represents this study guide, should you desire to order additional copies.

Item	Calif.*	Unit Price U.S.	B.C.*	Canada*	Quantity	Amount
FCF CS	$45.63	$42.55	$54.85	$51.25		$
FCF 1	6.76	6.30	8.95	8.50		
FCF 2	6.76	6.30	8.95	8.50		
FCF 3	6.76	6.30	8.95	8.50		
FCF 4	6.76	6.30	8.95	8.50		
FCF 5	6.76	6.30	8.95	8.50		
FCF 6	6.76	6.30	8.95	8.50		
FCF 7	6.76	6.30	8.95	8.50		
FCF SG	5.31	4.95	6.50	6.50		
					Subtotal	
				Overseas Residents *Pay U.S. price plus 10% surface postage or 25% airmail. Also, see "How to Order by Mail."*		
				U.S. First-Class Shipping *For faster delivery, add 10% for postage and handling.*		
				Gift to Insight for Living *Tax-deductible in the United States and Canada.*		
				Total Amount Due *Please do not send cash.*		$

If there is a balance: ❏ Apply it as a donation ❏ Please refund
*These prices already include applicable taxes and shipping costs.

Payment by: ❏ Check or money order payable to Insight for Living ❏ Credit card

(Circle one): Visa MasterCard Discover Card Number _____

Expiration Date _____ Signature _____
We cannot process your credit card purchase without your signature.

Name _____

Address _____

City _____ State/Province _____

Zip/Postal Code _____ Country _____

Telephone ( ) _____ Radio Station ____ ____ ____ ____
If questions arise concerning your order, we may need to contact you.

Mail this order form to the Ordering Services Department at one of these addresses:
Insight for Living, Post Office Box 69000, Anaheim, CA 92817-0900
Insight for Living Ministries, Post Office Box 2510, Vancouver, BC, Canada V6B 3W7
Insight for Living, Inc., GPO Box 2823 EE, Melbourne, VIC 3001, Australia